Cover image: "Portal". Original 16" X 20" oil on canvas painting by Todd Lorentz.

Cover designed by Cara Alexander-Brown.
Photo reproduction of original painting by www.spyd.ca.

Nagarjuna, Nondualism

and the

Nature of Nothing

By

Todd Lorentz

Vedanta Publishing
Edmonton, Canada

Nagarjuna, Nondualism and the Nature of Nothing.
Copyright © 2012
By Todd Lorentz

All rights reserved. Printed in the United States of America. No part of this book may be used or reproduced in any manner whatsoever without written permission except in the case of brief quotations embodied in critical articles and reviews.

All rights reserved
ISBN: 978-0-9877782-0-8

First Edition, January 2012

Author contact:
ToddLorentz@VedantaPublishing.com

Published by Vedanta Publishing
www.VedantaPublishing.com

This book is dedicated to
The World Teacher,
Whose Inspiration I
appreciate beyond words.

Table of Contents

Preface.. 1

Introduction... 7

1. Problems in Defining Nondualism........................ 21

2. Nonduality–The Negation of Dualist Thinking........ 45

3. Nonduality–The Nonplurality of the World............ 55

4. Nonduality–The Nondifference of Subject/Object... 67

5. Nonduality–The Identity of Phenomenon and the Absolute... 77

6. Nonduality–A Mystical Union Between the Individual and the Absolute............................. 85

7. Parallels between the *Mūlamadhyamakakārikā* and Quantum Physics..................................... 101

    Ontological Nonduality............................... 104

    Subject-Object Interdependence.................... 109

    The Two-Aspect Model of Reality................. 114

    The Tetralemma.. 119

Conclusion.. 127

Endnotes.. 133

Bibliography.. 145

Although not moving, the ONE is swifter than the mind;
the gods cannot catch it, as it speeds on in front.
Standing, it outpaces others who run;
within it Mātariśvan places the waters.

It moves—yet it does not move
It's far away—yet it is near at hand!
It is within this whole world—yet
it's also outside this whole world.

When a man sees all beings
within his very self,
and his self within all beings,
It will not seek to hide from him.

When in the self of a discerning man,
his very self has become all beings,
What bewilderment, what sorrow can there be,
regarding that self of him who sees this Oneness.

—Īśā Upanisad, verse 4-7

Preface

This particular work is the expression of a topic that is very close to my heart. From an early age I have experienced a fundamental sense of connectedness to both nature and other human beings. Despite the very personal yet superficial feelings that often accompanied me in the course of my typical adolescence, I could not help but revel in that sense of continuity between myself and the environment. My desire to understand this essential experience of interdependence and interconnectedness began there and, in some ways, has been a part of a driving motivation to understand the world and my place in it. The need to articulate this crucial aspect of my personal experience has led me on a fantastic and exciting journey and I have always chosen the risks in life over the comfort zones in an attempt to understand this phenomenon. Through this search I have come to understand that the most profound truths are often the simplest ones, although such simplicity is often difficult to see at first, and even more difficult to describe in a world intoxicated with complexity.

Of course, any philosophical view can become more agreeable once we come to terms with the *possibility* of its existence. Nondualism is such a view. Once I came to accept the possibility that my personal identity was responsible for an enormous distortion in my perception of reality, and that this same identity was not a fixed or permanent structure, I opened myself to an opportunity to understand and perceive reality in ways that were previously unimaginable. This is the charm, and some would say the curse, of exploring nonduality.

I came to discover that wherever I had entrenched some preconceived notion about the status of my being in the world, or the conditions of things around me, nondualism was there to confront my most basic assumptions with amazingly simple insights and solutions. From my earliest days of recollection I simply 'knew' intuitively that all things shared their very existence at some intimate and essential level. At present, nondualism has become, for me, a way to articulate that intuition.

Many difficulties can arise in any serious investigation of nondualism. The main problem, not surprisingly, involves the use of language for language is naturally dualistic in almost all its features and contexts. As soon as we begin to speak of nondualism we are constrained by the limits of presenting it dualistically. Some fields within the academic community, such as in physics or mathematics, have already made a great deal of progress in openly expressing nondualistic notions and, as we will see in chapter 7, some specialists within the field of quantum physics are already indicating that we should be imagining our place in nature in much more integral terms. This is exciting news for it suggests that we, as a species, are arriving at a place where we can rethink our current place in the world and re-order our lives in such a way as to reflect, and perhaps profoundly comprehend, an ontological place within the cosmos. That is to say, once we become socially conscious of our essential interdependence with each other and nature we can no longer order our relationships and interactions in the world on a model of competition or careless destruction. Instead, we will need to understand that the actions we may embark upon from moment to moment (whether physical, emotional, or mental) will have a direct effect upon the welfare of all. It requires that we develop a greater sense of responsibility toward all forms of life on this planet and, indeed, to life itself.

This process has already begun and we are seeing increasingly poignant expressions of behaviours throughout the world that are designed to heal our planet and our relationships to one another. More recently, with great movements under foot calling for justice, freedom, democracy and sharing, we are beginning to see the rise of a form of globalisation (of a positively cooperative nature) that represents a world truly beginning to reach out to one another on a mass scale. Unfortunately, our first political and economic models of globalisation were somewhat clumsy and immature, and have served more to perpetuate and intensify the suffering in the world than to alleviate it.

It is critical to our future that the greed and selfishness which has saturated the more recent iterations of corporate life does not become the export of the 21st century. My own optimism would assert that we are now beginning to make profound inroads toward a better global future, although much remains to be done. The essential barrier to more rapid progress, I believe, is due to the continuing and erroneous belief that we are essentially *separate* from one another, thus denying the responsibility that we naturally bear to one another and the world. Quantum physics has already established the fact that we are intimately connected with one another at the sub-atomic level. But old (mental) habits die hard and I expect that our deeply entrenched thoughtforms and beliefs about the divisions between each of us will persist for at least a short while yet; with an unfortunate prolonged suffering for *billions* of people on this planet.

In the meantime, it remains my desire to continue to articulate an understanding of nondualism for those who are looking for a language of nonduality through which to interpret and express their own similar intuitions. While a dualistic perspective has enabled us to make great sociological and technological gains, it will also lead us to extinction if we would continue to hold to the notions that it is the limit of our reality. This is most evident in the area of relationships between both individuals and nations and, as a result, we are witnessing enormous strains on both personal and international interactions around the world.

Many of the world's problems today can be traced to the one belief that we are separate from one another. This, if I might be so bold as to declare, is our "original sin" and is worth a considerable amount of thought and contemplation on our part. If the reader can imagine that this one belief could change, and it *must* change eventually, the world would quickly begin the work toward establishing a new expression of living in cooperation, sharing, and mutually supportive relations. As David Abram states so explicitly in the opening line of his book, *The Spell of the Sensuous*, "humans are tuned for relationship. The eyes, the skin, the tongue, ears, and nostrils—are all gates where our body receives the nourishment of otherness." It is a distressing reality, then, that those same senses distort our perception of reality so thoroughly as to give us the mistaken impression of separation. Even more painful is the irony that these same 'nourishing envoys of relationship' might play a part so central to ensuring that we generally fail so often in relationship from the selfish notions of separation that they engender. In a very real and pressing way we need to move beyond the restrictions that dualistic thinking imposes upon us and it should already have become apparent to us by now that our present paradigm sustains an ignoble existence for many. We ignore this knowledge at the risk of our survival on this planet.

It is my sincerest hope that, above all, the ideas presented in the following chapters will provide readers with a greater *personal* awareness and understanding of nondualist philosophy. It is hoped that such an understanding can eventually lead to a genuinely sincere experience of what is being described. Without such a personal experience, the human being will remain disconnected from its experience of true Joy, and the very Source of Life itself.

Todd Lorentz
December 21, 2011

Nagarjuna, Nondualism and the Nature of Nothing

Introduction

One of the more celebrated philosophers in Buddhist history is Nāgārjuna. This Indian saint, whose life during the 2nd century CE was said to have been foretold 500 years earlier by the Buddha himself, was responsible for the development of the philosophical school of thought that later became known as Mādhyamika Buddhism. It is generally agreed that Nāgārjuna's position was in support of an essentially nondualistic interpretation of reality, although he rarely ever expressed this ontological position explicitly. Instead, Nāgārjuna's dialectical method analyzed the epistemological distortions which arose for the thinker from approaching reality dualistically (i.e., in terms of a subject/object perspective). This was no more prevalent than in his well known treatise the *Mūlamadhyamakakārikā* (A Treatise on the Middle Way). The value of this particular treatise lay in how it was able to provide such detail on Nāgārjuna's central views. As Geoffrey Samuel stated:

> The Madhyamaka philosophy of Nāgārjuna and his followers is indeed an attempt to express the central insight of the Buddhist Enlightenment through a universalizing application of reason. It is also a culmination of the extensive philosophical developments both within and outside Buddhism over the previous centuries, and it bespeaks the dominance of literate, rationalized thinking in India at that time. It is a sustained attempt to use that mode of thinking against itself.[1]

Nāgārjuna uses his text to deconstruct the main philosophical and metaphysical positions of his time.

From the notions of essence, being, time, motion, and relation, to the ideas surrounding suffering, nirvāna, pratītya-samutpāda, tathāgata, the four noble truths, and agency, Nāgārjuna's dialectical methodology succeeded in undermining the arguments positing the "inherent existence of things" and, by extension, a dualistic approach to reason and experience.

While Nāgārjuna's approach throughout this work supported an essentially nondualistic view of reality, general analysis of his position has tended to focus mainly on the definitive and climactic conclusion he made surrounding the fundamental emptiness of our 'conventional' notions of reality. This analysis, while logically coherent, often failed to expose the finer features of his methodological process which appeared to build upon a series of ascending nondualist positions – each of which, within themselves, represented a definitive stage of nondual standing. The final three chapters of the *Mūlamadhyamakakārikā*, therefore, were often represented as embodying the conclusion of an argument that was developed throughout the previous twenty-four chapters, constituting in themselves a sort of preamble. While it is valid to view it in this way for certain tasks his work can also be seen as a collection of distinct aspects of nondualism which could represent more or less complete notions in themselves.

Edward Conze suggested that for the Mādhyamika conception of emptiness, "one of the most frequent synonyms is *Non-duality*."[2] While few would disagree with this interpretation, it is a significant generalization of Nāgārjuna's philosophical position. Conze provides little distinction on the various categories of nondualism which the Mādhyamikan philosophy makes available. On the other hand, G. M. Nagao provided a detailed exposition on the Buddhist principles underlying Nāgārjuna's nondualist system in order to clarify and express its subtleties to the western world. For example, in his work entitled *Mādhyamika and Yogācāra*, Nagao provided a fascinating look at the nuances present within the doctrine of emptiness (*śūnyatā*) and examined the complementary relationship between the two central and important schools of Mahāyāna thought. Notwithstanding his lucid and detailed analysis, however, even he failed to render the subtler categories of nondualism and places his primary emphasis on *śūnyatā* as the most important expression of Nāgārjuna's philosophy. As Nagao asserts:

> They [Yogācāra] complemented the [Mādhyamika] *śūnyatā* philosophy with various positive theories such as the theory of consciousness-only, the three-nature theory, the theory of Buddha's body, and so on. The Yogācāra theories are said to be "positive" because by accepting the negative idea of *śūnyatā* as a whole, the Yogācāra establishes the positive affirmative aspect of [the Mādhyamika] *śūnyatā* (abhāvasya bhāvah).[3]

For Nagao, the Mādhyamikan philosophy was, in reality, incomplete and "was brought to completion by the Yogācāra."[4] His emphasis then, understandably, was upon the doctrinal contributions bestowed upon Mādhyamika by its younger sibling Yogācāra rather than upon the subtle distinctions of nondualism within Mādhyamika itself.

It is important to further distinguish the fact that Nāgārjuna's dialectic is multi-layered, and that his succession of dialectic arguments are developed through a series of distinct and progressive forms of nondualism. These distinct forms work together to establish the larger philosophical system of nondualism known as the *doctrine of emptiness*. It is possible, therefore, to identify the characteristics in these various aspects of nondualism as they existed within his philosophical treatise. In doing so, a greater subtlety would be seen to be operating throughout the entirety of the *Mūlamadhyamakakārikā*.

With this in mind, I have developed an analysis of nondualism in Nāgārjuna's *Mūlamadhyamakakārikā* using a distinct system of nondualist categorization. My approach will utilize the five major aspects of nondualist interpretation developed in part by David Loy in his work, *Nonduality: A Study in Comparative Philosophy*. Drawing upon the features in these five aspects, we will be able to identify and demonstrate their frequency and expression within Nāgārjuna's *Mūlamadhyamakakārikā*, The particular translation that I will depend upon will be the version provided by Jay L. Garfield (1995),[5] and all references will include a chapter/verse reference for the reader's convenience.[6]

I will follow-up this analysis of multi-layered nondualism in Nāgārjuna's text with an examination of similar principles and concepts as they are found within the field of quantum physics. Through this assessment striking parallels will be seen to exist between the notions developed by Nāgārjuna and those outlined in the field of theoretical physics. It is through this comparison that we will be able to witness the degree of uniformity and parsimony that exists between these distinct nondualistic schemas.

The particular translation of the *Mūlamadhyamakakārikā* by Ray L. Garfield was chosen for use in this analysis after discussions with a variety of colleagues and mentors. Apart from his reputation as a recognized scholar in the field of Buddhist studies, Garfield has obviously capitalized on his study of previous translations and commentaries.[7] It is apparent in his analysis of the text that he has overcome many of the contradictions that have appeared in previous works.

These works, by order of their appearance, include translations by Frederick Streng (1967), Kenneth Inada (1970), a partial translation (17 of 27 chapters) by Mervyn Sprung (1979), and David Kalupahana (1986). Of these previous translations, Christian Lindtner says the following:

> The previous attempts of Inada, Streng and Sprung were, to say the least, not successful and though I am only too happy to say that Prof. Kalupahana's translations are seldom as bad as any of theirs, it is still bad--real bad.[8]

Given Lindtner's review of these prior works, and the confusion that any scholar of this topic has suffered after wading through the identified works above, Garfield's translation in 1995 emerged as a profoundly readable and clear-minded rendition of this important text.

Likewise, I found Garfield's commentaries to be some of the most lucid and penetrating descriptions that I have encountered in relation to the foundation concepts of nondualism. That is, Garfield is able to provide a coherent delineation of Nāgārjuna's subtle nondualist philosophy for the western philosophical mind. This particular translation and commentary also lends itself well to phenomenological analysis and, therefore, is particularly suited for use in this project.

I will begin my analysis in Chapter 1 by providing a working definition of nonduality. More than this, however, I will identify some points of historical interest surrounding this term and discuss the difficulty of even arriving at a definition. From one perspective, nonduality can be simplistically described (from the dualist perspective) as the opposite notion to duality. This, as we will come to see, is logically self-contradictory, if not incomplete. From another perspective, nonduality encompasses that state of experience which Buddhist texts described as Nirvāna, and to which other religious traditions have sometimes referred to with terms such as the Kingdom of Heaven, Enlightenment, Satori, the Absolute, the Tao, and many others. While it is true that these terms also refer to sometimes distinctly different concepts according to their own cultural roots, nevertheless, they individually partake in the root notion of nonduality.

The fundamental experience of nonduality is essentially unknowable and ineffable within the boundaries of traditionally dualistic paradigms. However, whilst embroiled within that material-world paradigm there exists a need within the human mind to cling to the use of dualistic terms and descriptions in order to reach some comprehension of the intuitive sense that there exists 'something' beyond the knowable (these initial descriptions, as you can well see, are rife with paradox, contradiction and, perhaps, irony. I therefore ask for the reader's patience until we can address the issue in more detail).

Either way, any definition that might be agreed upon will necessarily be insufficient to capture the full extent of nondualist thought. The use of any traditional term for nonduality will likely limit the breadth of understanding we might achieve about nondualist thought.

I have hoped to overcome some of the limitations of terminology by utilizing five progressively subtler notions or aspects of nondualism. In this way I will be able to paint a multidimensional "image" of nondualism in a way that doesn't specifically confine it to one concept or term, while covering a broad spectrum of nondualist perspectives or approaches at the same time. For all of my searching, Nāgārjuna's *Mūlamadhyamakakārikā*, to my mind, represents one of the best complete short works to contain all five of the major categories of nondualism. The progressive layers of advancing subtlety that is developed through these five categories is similarly reflected in the progressive arguments of Nāgārjuna's dialectic.

Chapter 2 begins my examination with the first aspect of nondualism – *the negation of dualistic thinking*. This section addresses the most basic of nondualistic claims and is commonly described as *advayavāda*, or the doctrine of 'not-two.' Ontological views of the world are commonly established through the exposition of bi-polar opposites: object/subject, being/non-being, life/death, etc. The logical problem, as Nāgārjuna will show, occurs when each half of the polarity is referred to as though it was a fully present subject, inherently existent and complete in itself. Nāgārjuna grounds his arguments in the 'Doctrine of Two Truths' and shows that it is our mistaken perception of the world, unthinkingly accepted as 'conventional truth', that perpetuates this relentless process of reification within the human mind. The negation of dualist thinking will also be examined through Nāgārjuna's use of the Tetralemma. This tool serves as a mechanism through which he might demonstrate the incoherence of dualistic thinking.

In chapter 3, I will identify the argument for the *nonplurality of the world* within Nāgārjuna's work. Here, Nāgārjuna makes use of the Buddhist *fivefold analysis* – itself an investigation of the very conception of *relationship* itself. This form of analysis suggests that a belief in the existence of 'relations' *itself* is incoherent and its endorsement leads to a vicious regress. This is made clearer through the logical arguments of F. H. Bradley, which serve to clarify and further substantiate a nondualistic understanding of reality.

In chapter 4, I will describe and identify an interesting aspect of nondualism that remains the central argument in many of the Eastern traditions – *the nondifference of subject and object*. As Loy seems to suggest, some of the philosophical positions found in the East start by collapsing the subject into the object, while others reverse this approach and collapse the object into the subject to achieve a common metaphysical position of ultimate oneness.[9] However, Nāgārjuna takes a more direct line of attack and discounts the ultimate existence of either. The important conclusion for Nāgārjuna is that neither the subject nor the object possesses inherent, autonomous existence. While it may be true to say that individuality arises temporarily or dependently, the claim cannot be further made that that existence, as a self-sufficient independent object, is true in the *ultimate* sense. The empirical material existence, for instance, that is witnessed as independent 'personhood,' is temporary and transient. It arises dependently upon other causes and conditions and possesses no *inherent* existence of its own. Nāgārjuna achieves this position in the *Mūlamadhyamakakārikā* through a long series of arguments that come together to establish the logical grounds for this aspect of nondualism. Throughout this stage of the dialectic, Nāgārjuna erodes the possibility for any essential existence of either the subject, the object, or, as mentioned in the previous category, any notion of a relationship between the two. All three aspects (subject, object, and the relationship between them) exist dependently, and arise upon conditions which are themselves dependently arisen. Nothing in the universe is completely independent of anything else.

In chapter 5, I identify the fourth aspect of nondualism within Nāgārjuna's dialectic – *the identity of phenomenon and the Absolute*. This constitutes a climactic moment of Nāgārjuna's work where he expresses the notion that "samsāra is nirvāna." According to Garfield's interpretation on this aspect of nondualism, individuals become emotionally and psychologically attached to their dualistic sensory interpretation of reality despite the fact that there is only one nondual reality. The issue, according to Nāgārjuna's argument, is that the belief in an independent existence for 'things' leads to an epistemological error in one's psychological interpretation of reality. Nondualism is the only logical ground that can be claimed despite what our sensory experience of the world dictates to our individual awareness. Release from this mistaken view requires mental training, discipline and a type of transcendent re-positioning of the consciousness (to step outside of the thinking mind) in order to move beyond the barriers imposed by dualistic thinking.

In chapter 6, I look at the logical and reasonable possibility that arises out of the first four aspects of nondualism. That is, that there exists *the possibility for the mystical union between the individual and the Absolute*. The *reality* of such a mystical union, much like Nāgārjuna's notions on ontological nonduality, cannot be explicitly asserted for to do so would be to continue to objectify or reify these terms as inherently existing things. However, the *possibility* of such a union is implied in his arguments in the conventional sense. In understanding the previous arguments laid out by Nāgārjuna, two major lines of reasoning will surface in regards to this aspect of nondualism.

First, views that idealize the notion of mystical union are views about things that have no inherent existence in the first place. All views are mere concepts that arise dependently within the mind. Therefore, it is possible for such a 'mystical union' to arise *in the conventional sense* because all conventional ideals have the possibility of arising dependently and temporarily.

Secondly, from the *ultimate point of view*, there never actually existed a separation between what was reified as the individual (subject) and what is referred to as the Absolute (object). It is only in the fact that individuals perceive themselves to be distinct and autonomous subjects that the experience of separation occurs, with the attendant emotional need to unite with what is conceptualized by that individual as the Absolute. It is through this self-created *experiential alienation* from the Absolute that a craving arises to re-unite with 'something' (i.e., some divine ground of being) and from which there was never really a separation in the first place. It is in coming to terms with the implications of this position that this final aspect is resolved. Nāgārjuna provides the arguments needed to resolve this dilemma.

That chapter will conclude the analysis of Nāgārjuna's *Mūlamadhyamakakārikā* within the parameters set by the five essential aspects of nondualism. Such an analysis serves to deliver a deeper understanding of the thoroughness and complexity of Nāgārjuna's dialectic. In the final chapter, this understanding will be seen to contribute to a greater appreciation of the emerging views in other contemporary topics — namely, quantum physics.

In chapter 7, the views expressed in Nāgārjuna's dialectic are compared against the newly emerging views in quantum physics. Such a comparison will bring to light striking parallels between these two distinct fields of thought. That they both deal with nondualist principles should come as no surprise. What is more astonishing, perhaps, is the congruence evidenced between the essential features and declarations of each. Given the integrity found within the structure of each system of thought, it should serve as an exciting submission that each would compare so favourably to the other.

One of the central practical applications of quantum physics is the occasion it provides to understand the root nature of the world in distinction to the reality that is commonly experienced. In a similar fashion, the *Mūlamadhyamakakārikā*, in its own period, represented the same practical search. As Samuel contends:

> Nāgārjuna's most important text, the *Mūlamadhyamakakārikā* or 'Root Verses of the Madhyamaka,' takes the fundamental terms of Indian philosophy and the Abhidharma in 27 short verse chapters. In a highly aphoristic style, Nāgārjuna examines each term in turn, demonstrating that it is incapable of yielding a consistent meaning. Once rational thought has been demonstrated to lead to a series of dead ends, the way is open for the attainment of direct insight into the nature of reality.[10]

Jaidev Singh explains the important role that the *Mūlamadhyamakakārikā* played as a vehicle for Nāgārjuna's philosophical position, as well as its role in Buddhist philosophy:

> Practically all the basic concepts of Nāgārjuna's philosophy are found in the Kārikā...[and] Nāgārjuna has all along used the technique of *prasanga vākya*, argument or *reductio ad absurdum* character. His main concern is to expose the absurdities involved in accepting what is only relative (nihsvabhāva) as absolute (sasvabhāva). Even in the Kārikā, Nāgārjuna avers with unmistakable forthrightness that the conditioned bespeaks the unconditioned as its ultimate ground.[11]

Introduction

D. S. Ruegg described the degree to which Nāgārjuna's work influenced a variety of Buddhist schools and their leading thinkers. He provided an impressive list of writers known to have supplied commentaries on the *Mūlamadhyamakakārikā* which included: Ch'ing-mu, Buddhapālita, Candrakīrti, Bhāvaviveka, Devaśarman, Gunaśri, and Rāhula, as well as members from the Yogācārin/Vijñānavādin school like Asanga, Sthiramati, and Gunamati.[12] As Ruegg observed:

> The existence of such commentaries on the MMK by leading authorities of the Vijñānavāda clearly indicates that Nāgārjuna's work was not considered to be the exclusive property of the Mādhyamikas in the narrow sense of a particular school, and that it was regarded as fundamental by Mahāyānist thinkers of more than one tendency.[13]

It should be of no surprise that this work had an enormous effect in the East on philosophy. It should be even less of a surprise that it can still wield a tremendous power of influence on our thinking today as well as serve to prepare our minds for the new paradigm that is emerging into our awareness in this century.

19

Nagarjuna, Nondualism and the Nature of Nothing

Problems in Defining Nondualism

Before this analysis of the *Mūlamadhyamakakārikā* can begin, it is necessary to develop a working definition of *subject-object nondualism*. This is perhaps one of the most difficult of concepts to define as language itself is dualistic by nature and, therefore, insufficient to provide a complete picture. According to Garfield, Nāgārjuna's use of a reasoning device known as the Tetralemma indicates just how difficult it can be to deal with this concept through the use of definitive language or terminology. As Garfield notes:

> We see that when things are plausibly posited by an interlocutor as ultimates, Nāgārjuna resorts to a negative tetralemma. This emphasizes that all discourse is only possible from the conventional point of view. When we try to say something coherent about the nature of things from an ultimate standpoint, we end up talking nonsense.[14]

To make matters even more difficult, the essential characteristic of the nondualist experience is that it is dualistically featureless (i.e., lacking in subject-object distinctions) and is beyond our traditional conceptual and epistemological frameworks. We can speak conceptually of subject-object nondualism and employ linguistic markers as descriptions of nondualism, however, we are always faced with the paradox that "we" (the subject) are dualistically describing a "thing" (the object) that, in its most intimate form, lacks the subject-object poles of reference. Therefore, it is important to be aware of the fact that we are dealing with a term (i.e., nondualism) that is intended to refer to what is, in the end, indescribable. An entirely academic or intellectual conception of nonduality will leave us short of the broader meaning of Nāgārjuna's work as interpreted by such scholars as Conze, Loy, Kalupahana, Garfield, or Nagao. As Christian Lindtner points out, Nāgārjuna expected that a full understanding of the meaning of nondualism would come about through the integration of that concept into one's own experience. There existed the expectation that the disciple had already prefaced their reading of the text with years of meditation and personal critical reflection upon the essence of nondualism and emptiness.[15] The goal of reading such a treatise on emptiness, according to Paul Hacker, was to achieve release or liberation and the reader was expected to integrate this knowledge into their actual perception of reality.[16] "In Indian philosophy knowledge is never an end in itself, but always serves the purpose of liberation."[17] However, this should not deter us from pursuing an academic or intellectual understanding of nondualism for it is only in doing so that such a deeper integration might ever occur.

For the purpose of clarity, I have tried to employ the use of language that serves to directly describe nonduality and/or nondual experience in a way which stimulates an intuitive response to the notions being presented. For that reason, some phrases may be repeated or constructed in a manner that might appear linguistically clumsy. While this clumsiness is certainly avoidable, the use of such devices can serve to carry forward thoughts that normally appear to contradict dualist conceptions or mental conditionings. Articulating nondualism seems to me to require a special skill of which I am only now becoming aware. Rather than creating a mental concept of it in the mind, which often results through the use of positive language, an understanding of nondualism can be developed through overcoming the dualistic view of having a separate 'self' or *permanently* distinct existence in the world. This requires more de-construction of our thinking rather than construction and is sometimes accomplished through the use of subjective language. Subjective language, while generally less desirable to employ than objective language within the context of an academically styled thesis, can assist in drawing the reader to identify closer with the point being written about. The reader's own identity will then, to some degree, become vulnerable to the same de-constructive influences imposed in subsequent stages of de-constructive analysis. While the use of objective language can help in developing an intellectual comprehension of nondualism, subjective language can add a further dimension to one's experience.

In the case of Garfield's translation of the *Mūlamadhyamakakārikā*, we can see that Nāgārjuna alternates between both the subjective and objective tones in his writing. For example, in chapter XXI entitled "Examination of Becoming and Destruction," Nāgārjuna engages in a decidedly objective analysis of the concepts of becoming and destruction up to verse 10. He begins by objectively examining the inconsistencies and ephemeral nature discerned in the processes of becoming and destruction, and concludes that it is simply illogical to attribute independent or distinct existence to such phenomena. In verse 11, however, he retreats from this objective tone and engages directly with the reader in a way that forces the reader to question their perceptions and to identify with his analysis:

> If you think you see both
> Destruction and becoming,

> Then you see destruction and becoming
> Through impaired vision.
> (chapter XXI, verse 11)[18]

Following this verse, he again returns to his objective tone through the remaining verses of analysis on this topic. This device is direct, yet effective.

Therefore, a distinctly subjective tone may appear in some sections of this thesis with the intent of developing a richer understanding of nondualism. In the case of nondualism itself, the academic community may eventually find the need to forego the strictly intellectual approach of "objective analysis" in some empirical studies and to include some measure of intimate engagement with the text, much the same as Nāgārjuna has done here, in order to develop new levels of insight.[19]

The conception of nondualism stretches back to earlier Vedic writings such as the Ramayana. While little in the way of a distinctly nondual doctrine is actually openly described, the early Vedic tradition contained many references to concepts like Ultimate Reality and *Brahman*, and which were used in a decidedly nondualistic sense. Erich Frauwallner suggests that the introduction of world-origination or creation doctrines raised the first real ontological questions regarding monism/idealism.[20] This was particularly evident during the Upanishadic era and the rise of early Buddhism around the 6th century BCE.[21] At that time, a considerable attempt was made by many philosophical groups to express the nature of reality. Some developed their philosophical positions in a distinctly dualistic framework, while others sought to define ultimate reality within nondualistic terms. According to the Dhammapada:

> "All created things are grief and pain," he who knows and sees this becomes passive in pain; this is the way that leads to purity.
> "All forms are unreal," he who knows and sees this becomes passive in pain; this is the way that leads to purity.
> (*The Dhammapada*, verse 278, 279)[22]

If the earliest teachings of the Buddha, as denoted in the passage above, denied the basic independence and reality of forms then we already have evidence of an early push toward a monism of sorts. At the very least, it eschews the path of reification (i.e. "All *created* things are grief and pain") and emphasizes that an understanding of the temporality of the world of forms can 'purify' the mind and release one from pain and suffering. The passage also suggests that early Buddhist teachings held the experiences of separation and dualism to be mistaken views that lie at the root of all suffering. Either way, it seemed to be a time of great intellectual capacity and growth.

The arrival of Nāgārjuna in the 2nd century CE, and Āryāsanga in the 4th–5th century CE, brought a further development to the nondualist facet of the Buddhist tradition. For example, Nāgārjuna provided a complete system of nondualistic philosophical meaning that responded well to the philosophical challenges of the time. While literary works of these two Buddhist scholars present us with what appears to be uniquely original nondualist expositions on reality, E. Obermiller suggests that "the ideas expressed in these two branches of Mahāyāna are much older than Āryāsanga and Nāgārjuna who have only established regular philosophical systems."[23] This statement points to an attempt on the part of these thinkers to organize the various schools of thought that had arisen centuries earlier. For the purposes of this analysis, Nāgārjuna represents one of the more important instances in the development of a comprehensive nondualist philosophical doctrine. As D.S. Ruegg suggests:

> In view of his place in the history of Buddhist thought and because of his development of the theory of the non-substantiality and emptiness of all *dharmas*, it seems only natural to regard Nāgārjuna as one of the first and most important systematizers of Mahāyānist thought.[24]

In other areas of the east, similar schools of thought developed variations on the nondualist theme. As early as the 6th century BCE in China, Lao Tzu was said to have expressed the essence of the *Tao-te ching* through *wu-wei*, or non-action.[25] Non-action, in this context, meant "taking no action that is contrary to Nature"[26] and comes about through the complete identification and unity with Nature and its processes. This natural action, or acting in harmony with Nature without effort, is qualified further by Loy and he provides a key insight to the problem:

> The root irruption and disturbance of the natural order of things is man's self-consciousness, and the return to Tao is conversely a realization of the ground of one's being, including one's own consciousness. If consciousness of self is the ultimate source of unnatural action, then natural action must be that in which there is no such self-consciousness—in which there is now awareness of the agent as being distinct from "his" act.[27]

This meaning was often implied, more than stated outright, within the *Tao-te ching*. However, as Loy suggests, the natural expression and movement in life, which is at the heart of Taoist teaching, was likely to be achieved only in the absence of a self-conscious awareness of agent and action. In this sense, we can already see some similarities with Nāgārjuna's deconstruction of the agent and action in chapter VIII:

> Action depends upon the agent.
> The agent itself depends on action.
> One cannot see any way
> To establish them differently.
> (chapter VIII, verse 12)[28]

For Nāgārjuna, both the 'agent' and the 'action' are mutually dependent and can not be said to have individual inherent existences. One part simply cannot exist without the other. Not unlike Loy's interpretation of *wu-wei*, where the agent no longer exists (i.e., no longer has self-conscious existence), so too does *intentional* action cease and becomes 'actionless-action' or 'non-action'.

Similarly, the notions of nonduality were exemplified in the various Hindu systems known as Vedānta. The most famous of these schools was promoted by the Indian master Śankara, around the 8th century CE, and was known as Advaita Vedānta.[29]

> Advaita Vedānta holds that only pure spirit or consciousness—called Ātman, Brahman, the Highest Ātman, the Highest Brahman, even the highest Lord—truly exists. The plurality of individual souls is illusory; only the universal Self is real. The essence of the self is described as

> light of knowledge and subsistent bliss. It is one, simple, and without parts. It never changes: every form of becoming, be it birth, change, activity, or suffering, is foreign to it. The bliss, knowledge, and being that comprise its nature are one and the same.[30]

Interestingly enough, Hacker also sees this position as having its roots grounded in notions derived from earlier Buddhist schools of thought.

> The philosophical basis of this radical monism [Advaita Vedānta] is an illusionism (*māyāvāda*) which is, in part, derived from the illusionism of later Buddhism—the schools of relativism (*śūnyavāda*) or Madhyamaka and epistemological idealism (*vijñānavāda*) or Yogācāra. If only the One Consciousness is real, it is argued, then everything in our experience that is multiple, changing, and material—the entirety of phenomenal experience—is not truly real. Unreal, however, does not mean *nonexistent*.[31]

At about the same period as the rise in popularity of Śaṅkara's Advaita instruction, from about the 7th to the 13th century CE, surprisingly similar notions were being developed and preserved by a now extinct Tibetan Buddhist school of ontological investigators called the *Jo nan pas*. Ruegg refers to this group as holding an "extreme and somewhat isolated position"[32] which, although quite un-Buddhist in some aspects, taught "a theory of the absolute Gnosis..., undifferentiated between apprehender and apprehended..., which is constant or permanent...and 'substantially' real...and which is the *parinispanna* or Absolute."[33]

While the *Jo nan pas* considered themselves to be the true preservers of the Mādhyamika philosophy, many Tibetans who followed Candrakīrti's commentaries opposed them vehemently.[34] Obermiller even referred to them once as the 'brahmanists' in Tibet, although this view is not widely held.[35]

Speculations on Nondualism were no less common in the West and the possibility exists that the early Greeks may have encountered eastern influences early on in their philosophical development. J. F. Staal provides a significant appendix in his book *Advaita and Neoplatonism* documenting "the probability of actual communications"[36] between the Greeks and the East Indians. Likewise, he recalls Porphyry's account of the effort made by Plotinus to 'learn directly the philosophy practiced among the Persians and that which was held in esteem among the people of India,"[37] although this can hardly be considered conclusive evidence of cultural and philosophical exchange between the two.

Whether they were influenced directly by Eastern philosophers or not it is unmistakable that the Western philosophical tradition had also developed its own distinct expression of nondualism. From Greek thinkers such as Pythagorus, Parmenides, and Plotinus, to the later philosophical positions of Scotus, Spinoza, Hegel, Bradley, and Whitehead, nondualism and monistic idealism has continued to challenge and influence the Western worldview.

This discussion is in no way intended to represent a comprehensive historical view of nondualism in the East, nor a comprehensive overview of nondualism itself. Nevertheless, it does indicate the rich and prolific presence of nondualist ideals throughout the history of Asian culture, and Nāgārjuna's work provides a significant contribution to that collection of nondualist philosophy in the East.

Nāgārjuna was a 2nd century Indian philosopher who, it is believed, originated from South India – perhaps near Vidarbha.[38] He left home at a young age and came upon Nalanda University where he took up studies and eventually became the head of that esteemed institute. Murty suggests that around 24 major works have been ascribed to Nāgārjuna,[39] although Buddhist scholars, such as Christian Lindtner, suggest that we can only be certain of a few.[40] The *Mūlamadhyamakakārikā* was chief amongst these.[41]

> As indicated in the very title, 'The fundamental verses on the Middle (Way)' called 'Wisdom,' the large number of important commentaries by renowned teachers, and thirdly, by its very thorough and radical treatment of the cardinal concepts (*dharma*) of Buddhist systematic soteriology (Abhidharma), MK [the *Mūlamadhyamakakārikā*] may suitably be labeled the *chef d'oeuvre* among Nāgārjuna's dialectical tracts.[42]

Garfield suggests that a thorough understanding of the Doctrine of Two Truths is vital in interpreting Nāgārjuna's philosophical position. This is important to grasp as it is this doctrine that provides the foundation upon which Nāgārjuna grounds much of his dialectic. In fact, little coherence will be found throughout the *Mūlamadhyamakakārikā* without an understanding of this important Mādhyamika principle (as was evidenced in some later Western translations).

Reality consists of two fundamental aspects – *conventional truth* and *ultimate truth*. Garfield explains:

> There is a conventional world of dependently arisen objects and properties, of selves and their properties and relations. And there in that world there is conventional truth: Snow is white. Grass is green. Individual humans are distinct from one another and from their material possessions. But there is also an ultimate truth about this world: It is empty (of inherent existence). None of these objects or persons exists from its own side (independently of convention). From the ultimate point of view there are no individual objects or relations between them.[43]

There is the actual world, as it exists in itself (*ultimate reality*), in which no distinct independent, autonomous, or self-existent entities subsist. Even more important, if the perception of individual objects is an illusion then the relationships between them must also be illusory. This is an important point to consider and will be addressed in more detail in subsequent chapters.

Ultimate reality, or reality-as-it-is, is nondual. Yet, there also exists the individual's epistemological interpretation of conventional reality in which the world *appears* as an assembly of distinct objects and properties and in which *seemingly* autonomous subjects appear to exist and interact. Nagao suggests that:

> Conventional truth refers to ordinary truth established by the logic and concept common in the mundane and public world. Ultimate truth refers to truth that is revealed when the logic and concept of the ordinary, common, mundane, and public world has been transcended. It is truth that

is 'inexpressible' through ordinary language and that is 'inconceivable' by ordinary logic.[44]

Edward Conze describes the Mahāyāna view of ultimate reality as "the Absolute in its emptiness."[45] The world, as it is generally perceived, is a dualistic panorama of 'is' and 'is not.' Emptiness transcends these polarized positions by recognizing the inherent nondual nature of the Absolute.

> 'It is,' is one extreme; 'it is not' is another. Between these two limits the world is imprisoned. The holy men transcend this limitation. Avoiding both extremes, the Tathagata teaches a Dharma in the middle between them, where alone the truth can be found. This Dharma is now called *emptiness*. The Absolute is emptiness and all things also are empty. In their emptiness Nirvana and the world coincide, they are no longer different but the same.[46]

Indeed, ultimate reality, from the Mahāyāna Buddhist perspective, is essentially nondual. We are tempted, partly due to our sensory conditioning and partly due to our use of language, to polarize our views of the twofold truth – naturally, it is the line of least resistance to assign actual existence to one (i.e., ultimate truth) and non-existence or illusory existence to the other (i.e., conventional truth). Nāgārjuna explicitly rejects this temptation. Paul Williams provides his distinctive exposition on the Two-Truths doctrine and gives us a closer idea of what Nāgārjuna appears to have intended:

> Conventional and ultimate are not two distinct realities, two realms opposed to each other. It should be clear that the ultimate, emptiness, is what is ultimately the case concerning the object

under investigation. It is what makes the object of a conventional entity and not an ultimate one, as we think it is. Emptiness makes the conventional conventional. Conventional and ultimate are thus not separate. Nevertheless, they are also not the same. A chair and its emptiness of inherent existence are not literally the same thing, as is sometimes stated in modern books on Madhyamaka. The fact that something lacks inherent existence is not just a way of looking at that thing. It is also something which happens to be true of it as well![47]

The notions themselves, of conventional truth and ultimate truth, are equally real – or more accurately, equally empty. The *Mūlamadhyamakakārikā* constitutes an effort at undermining this dualistic tendency in thinking.

> By distinguishing the conventional from the ultimate, it is tempting to disparage the former in contrast to the latter, developing a sort of theory of one truth and one falsehood. This is done if one reifies the entities associated with the ultimate, such as emptiness or impermanence, or the Four Noble Truths, or the Buddha. Then one treats these as real, intrinsically existent phenomena. The conventional then becomes the world of illusion.[48]

The dangers of engaging in discourse about the ultimate nondual reality are becoming clear. In attempting to define or describe states that are essentially ineffable, the risk of cultivating a sense of essential reality about them can arise which leads to further incoherence, paradox and self-contradiction. Likewise, the difficulty in providing a particular set of definitions for nonduality is becoming more apparent. The more precise the definition of nonduality becomes, the more it is 'dualized' and the further we seem to get from actually encompassing its meaning. Garfield reveals:

> Ultimate truth is, in some sense, ineffable in that all words and their referents are by definition conventional. The dualities generated by the use of terms that denote individuals or classes as distinct from others or from their complements are unavoidable in discourse and nonexistent in the ultimate.[49]

So what can we make of the term *nondualism*? This word is intended to describe reality as it 'truly' is, devoid of the boundaries between the 'self' and 'other,' and within which we form our subjective interpretations of the world around us. An understanding of the term nondualism requires a movement of the mind that is outside of its dualistically conditioned paradigm. Loy explains:

> No concept is more important in Asian philosophical and religious thought than *nonduality* (Sanskrit *advaya* and *advaita*, Tibetan *gÑis-med*, Chinese *pu-erh*, Japanese *fu-ni*), and none is more ambiguous. The term has been used in many different although related ways, and to my knowledge the distinctions between these meanings have never been fully clarified.[50]

We are on uneasy ground here because we are dealing with a term that has been used to describe the true nature of reality; a reality which only a select group of mystics and saints, throughout all of history, have even claimed to have directly experienced or attained.

The notion of a nondual reality – of which the average dualistically conditioned mind is not sufficiently able to rationally conceive – is found in many places throughout Mādhyamika and Yogācāra literature. As Loy asserts, "the nondual nature of reality is indubitably revealed only in what they term enlightenment or liberation (*nirvāna, mōksa, satori*, etc), which is the experience of nonduality."[51] This enlightenment experience is often the result of a de-conditioning effort on the part of the practitioner, and volumes of literature on the method and means to achieve this state have been written. The essential stimulus toward encountering a nondual experience seems to involve a reordering and decentralization of one's mental environment in such a way that the individual is no longer constrained to interpret the world from an *egocentric* or *ego-existent* standpoint. In this sense, nondualism seems to be nearly impossible to define as it now encompasses everything and yet, mysteriously, it seems unable to refer to any one *thing* in particular.

The search for a satisfying and complete definition for nondualism appears to be a near impossible endeavor; the *entirety* of nondualism seems to lie outside of our dualistic interpretation of reality. It would be unattainable to render a *complete* formulation for nondualism. Nevertheless, it is important that such an attempt to define nondualism be made even though it falls short of the reality and can only take us to the frontier of nondualistic perception itself. Like the Zen koan, it provides the necessary tension and direction through which the mind might search for, and perhaps even experience, a true sense of the nondual reality. Without that tension one is apt to remain within the dualistic framework of interpreting reality. Therefore, an attempt at developing a definition will provide the necessary template from which to proceed in our analysis of the *Mūlamadhyamakakārikā*, as long as we continue to maintain our awareness of the fact that we will always be faced with the limitations described earlier.

On this last point, Loy reiterates the argument that nonduality is necessarily difficult to understand. "If we did understand it fully we would be enlightened, which is not understanding in the usual sense: it is the experience of nonduality that philosophizing obstructs."[52]

The push to understand nonduality is a two-edged sword that works both to unite and, at the same time, to intensify the split between subject and object. On the one hand, we seek to intellectually grasp the meaning of nonduality. In this regard, we employ clever mental tools to manipulate our understanding toward a philosophical conclusion that satisfies the limits of our perceptual framework. On the other hand, it is that conceptualized intellectual framework *itself* that serves as the obstacle to actually experiencing nondual reality. Once again Loy reminds us that:

> From such a perspective, the problem with philosophy is that its attempt to grasp nonduality conceptually is inherently dualistic and thus self-defeating. Indeed, the very impetus to philosophy may be seen as a reaction to the split between subject and object: philosophy originated in the need of the alienated subject to understand itself and its relation to the objective world it finds itself in.[53]

In that respect, *all* philosophy must, perchance, start with a caveat. We will not be able to achieve a full understanding of nondualism through philosophy and analysis alone. Furthermore, this project constitutes, perhaps for all of us, some aspect of our own personal search for integration and wholeness in the universe. As we have seen so far, that search cannot end here: it extends beyond the reach of language. According to the dictates of many nondualist systems, "philosophy cannot grasp the source from which it springs and so must yield to praxis: the intellectual attempt to grasp nonduality conceptually must give way to various meditative techniques which, it is claimed, promote the immediate experience of nonduality."[54]

As Christian Lindtner argues, the writings by Nāgārjuna lay a great deal of emphasis on *prajñā* (wisdom) and he relies on what Buddhist thinkers maintain are the three principal means to verify the accuracy of any statement – *śruti* (correct understanding of the scriptures), *cinta* (well-reasoned appraisal of the results of one's study), and *bhāvanā* (ultimately integrating one's learning into oneself) – to bring the reader to the desired understanding.[55]

> So to Nāgārjuna *prajñā* is at the outset a critical faculty constantly engaged in analyzing the more or less common-sense notions presented to it by tradition or experience. The more it penetrates them and 'loosens them up' the more their apparent nature vanishes and in the final analysis their true nature turns out to be 'empty', i.e., devoid of substance, or simply illusory as it cannot really be determined as A or, for that matter, non-A. At this stage *prajñā* has also brought its own raison d'être to an end: by analyzing its objects away it has also deprived itself of an objective support.[56]

Not only was the early student of the *Mūlamadhyamakakārikā* required to follow through with a rigorous analysis of the text but, according to Lindtner, Nāgārjuna expected the student to meditate on it in such a fashion as to integrate this new understanding into their very own individual perception of reality.[57] The reader needed to integrate this knowledge to such a degree as to actually *become it*. It is not enough to simply understand nonduality *intellectually*. One must come to *perceive* the world nondually through, or beyond, the mind. That few achieve this stage of *prajñā* is certain, yet it speaks to the fact that an intellectual understanding alone is insufficient to grasp the entirety of Nāgārjuna's views of the nondual Absolute. Even less so would be an attempt to define it *conclusively* for the reader.

Despite the seeming futility in formulating a definitive meaning for subject-object nondualism, the author of the *Mūlamadhyamakakārikā* has made specific assertions that necessarily affect our conceptual understanding of nondualism. These assertions constitute the background for this project. In analyzing the work of this 2nd century Indian philosopher, perhaps we may come to a better understanding of the subtleties of nondualism as a whole and move closer to an understanding of our essential relationships within reality.

The philosophy of Nāgārjuna is subtle and much more complex than what can be described in the analysis to follow. Indeed, the categories and questions raised by Nāgārjuna span the range of topics including metaphysics, epistemology, ontology, ethics, soteriology, and meta-philosophy. It is perhaps fitting at this juncture, then, to establish the parameters of investigation – the five major aspects of nondualism – which my analysis of this Buddhist text will undergo. It is my contention that a specific definition for nondualism can be substituted by an outline that contains a variety of aspects which develop for the reader a progressively comprehensive understanding of nonduality. What follows constitutes a working definition for the notion of nonduality.

In his work *Nonduality: A Study In Comparative Philosophy*, David Loy delineates five principal approaches to nonduality. These five aspects will form the standard and template for my identification of the corresponding incidences of nondualism within Nāgārjuna's *Mūlamadhyamakakārikā*. Taken together, they impart to us a working impression, a multidimensional image if you will, of nondualism. Admittedly, it may be possible to formulate additional categories of nondualism but, as Loy admits, "most of them can be subsumed under one or more of the...[five] categories."[58] The five aspects of nondualism, portrayed by Loy, and on which I will base my subsequent analysis of the *Mūlamadhyamakakārikā*, can be elaborated as follows:

1). *The negation of dualistic thinking* – The illogic of thinking in dualistic terms is demonstrated by the fact that whenever you forward one idea (i.e., light), you necessarily engage with its bi-polar opposite (i.e., dark). The reality of alternative views is denied here and can be described by the term *advayavāda* (the doctrine of not twofold, reality is not twofold).

2). *The nonplurality of the world* – The world of distinct phenomena (including the reification of oneself as a subject) is considered to consist of merely attributes or appearances of one nondual whole – defined variously as the Absolute, One Mind, and even *dharmadhātu*. These appearances of individual phenomena are considered to be illusions and arise dependently due to the way our senses register the world.

3). *The nondifference of subject and object* – An actual recognition of ourselves, as distinct and autonomous *subjects*, is an illusion. Various philosophical positions will often negate this duality by collapsing one pole of the opposites into the other. For example, the early Buddhist doctrine of *Anātman* (or 'no-self') collapsed the subject into the object (i.e., all existence is Buddha Mind or the Absolute); in Vedānta, the reverse is often the case and the object is more or less collapsed into the subject, or Self (i.e., everything is *Atman*). This type of nonduality is more clearly defined as *advaitavāda* (the doctrine of the nonduality of subject and object).

4). *The identity of phenomenon and the Absolute* – This category of nonduality is really an amalgamation of the first three types and alludes to the epistemological errors present in our perception of reality. David Loy refers to this type as "the nonduality of duality and nonduality" and is exemplified by the "claim that samsāra is nirvāna."[59] There is only one world but we may experience that world in alternative (illusory) ways. The actual claim here is that the distinctions between phenomenon and the Absolute are conceptual and empirical, although not *actual*.

5). *The possibility of a mystical union between the individual and the Absolute*[60] – If there are 'not two,' and if the previous aspects of nondualism hold true, then it is illogical to posit an ontological distinction between what we consider to be the divine creative force of the universe (i.e., the Absolute) and the individual, or individual phenomenon. One who has achieved *prajñā* (nondual wisdom) has gone beyond the distinctions of samsāra and nirvāna – thus, essentially uniting with the Absolute.

In this last instance, it would be incorrect to collapse one representation into the other such that an individual might be able to consider their *personal* self to be 'God', or in some way to think that they personally embody the Absolute. Similarly, it would be incorrect to say that the Absolute exists entirely within the mind of the individual or that the Absolute could be somehow anthropomorphized to resemble the limits in human understanding. Rather, for Nāgārjuna, both the individual and the Absolute are understood to be *conceptual* manifestations representing one or another of the illusory poles within *one nondual whole*. As the illusion of independent, inherent existence is seen, nirvāna arises and becomes apparent.

Curiously enough, each individual aspect of nondualism employs a negation of dualism in *some* form in order to make its point. This is due, in part, to the fact that we always move closer to an understanding of nondualism as we *remove* the various distinctions that arise in conventional dualistic perception. When we speak of nondualism in a positive categorical way it becomes more dualistically objectified and thus more distinct as merely one intellectual concept among many. The use of the negation counteracts this tendency and works toward dissolving the categories of opposites rather than implementing new ones. Nagao affirms that "the height to which Nagarjuna's philosophy developed the negative reasoning of emptiness is unparalleled in the history of philosophy."⁶¹ His dialectic of negation is present throughout the *Mūlamadhyamakakārikā*.

We will come to see the value of negation as it is used throughout Nāgārjuna's text, and my analysis throughout the subsequent chapters will look periodically at the ways in which he employs negation for each aspect of nondualism. He avoids making positive claims about the nature of reality and uses the various forms of negation (listed above) to begin dismantling the dualistic biases of the reader. This approach progressively clears one's internal mental landscape of conceptual objects that previously served to hinder any understanding of nondual reality. A categorically positive narrative on nondualism would have resulted in an ultimate contradiction between Nāgārjuna's method and his goal. As Bhattacharya stated:

> Nāgārjuna's Absolute is neither the world nor apart from the world. It is the 'intrinsic nature' of the world. But to say 'It is the intrinsic nature of the world', is to make of it an object, standing in relation, on the one hand, to the thinking subject, and on the other, to other objects, and thus to deprive it of its all-encompassing character. The only way in which Nāgārjuna can speak of it (or, rather, *out of* it) is to say: 'All things in the world are devoid of an intrinsic nature', i.e., the things in the world are not as they appear to us.⁶²

In this last statement, Bhattacharya gives us some idea of the subtle line Nāgārjuna must walk in his dialectical method. Throughout his arguments, Nāgārjuna is quite aware of the Absolute as the goal of understanding. To speak of it directly, however, reduces the Absolute to an objective state that is limited by the very act of conceptualization. As Bhattacharya concedes, "Nāgārjuna strives to express the Inexpressable,"[63] and this brings with it certain dangers for those attempting to penetrate into this mystery.

> Even during the time of Nāgārjuna, Buddhist thinkers were aware of the danger inherent in emptiness, of people mistaking it for a nihilistic view (*nāsti-vāda*) that would negate all human work and effort.... Nāgārjuna himself warned that 'a mistaken view of emptiness will destroy an unwise person, as surely as an ineptly handled poisonous snake.'[64]

Each individual aspect of nondualism illustrates a unique approach to the understanding of nondualism. However, each is insufficient on its own to encompass the entire range of nondual possibilities. A balanced approach, which includes an understanding of each of these aspects, will prevent the extremes of nihilism or self-contradiction and paradox. It is through the identification and use of these successively argued aspects of nondualism that that balance can be struck.

Nagarjuna, Nondualism and the Nature of Nothing

Nonduality – The Negation of Dualist Thinking

This first aspect of nonduality necessarily involves the notion that it is logically incoherent to utilize dualist terms as a way of establishing an ultimate metaphysical standpoint. The existence of "alternate views", or *advayavāda* (the doctrine of 'not twofold'), is denied here. As Loy explains, dualistic thinking is:

> thinking which differentiates that-which-is-thought-about into opposed categories: being and nonbeing, success and failure, life and death, enlightenment and delusion, and so on...we cannot take one without the other since they are interdependent: in affirming one half of the duality we maintain the other as well.[65]

The human mind, conditioned by its sensory relationship to the world, is overwhelmed by the subjective experience of that reality. This immersion into sensual experience is relatively consistent in its effects upon the human perspective. For the most part, we all experience the world *as* a distinct subjective being, having little sense of any practical or essential unity with other objects. This experience is inherently isolating in its effects and the essential qualitative characteristic of the subjective experience is alienation and *lack*.[66] Christmas Humphreys attempts to paint a picture of how this process ensues:

> The lower mind sees all things separate; the higher knows that they are forms of the same Reality. Desire, in the sense of a craving for the interests of the petty self is born of illusion, the illusion that the things desired are other than itself. Hatred, the father of all war and of most human suffering, follows on its train.

> To integrate these warring factors is the aim of mind control. Only a higher faculty than 'higher' and 'lower' thought can bring about synthesis, and this is Buddhi, the 'intuition' of Western psychology, the instrument of direct as distinct from indirect cognition, whereby the mind is enabled to rise above the state of knowing about the object of its thought, and to know it by a process of fusion which amounts to identity.[67]

It is in overcoming the tendencies of the 'lower' subjective material mind, and achieving a degree of *identification*, that the sense of separation can be overcome. Despite the widespread and pervasive presence of individual self-reification, Nāgārjuna asserts that this subjective separative perspective is a mistaken view of reality. Moreover, it is incoherent to describe anything within the world of objective phenomena in terms of *inherent existence*. All features arise dependently and no-*thing* can essentially exist independently.

> We say that the unpleasant
> Is dependent upon the pleasant,
> Since without depending on the pleasant there is none.
> It follows that the pleasant is not tenable.
>
> We say that the pleasant
> Is dependent upon the unpleasant.
> Without the unpleasant there wouldn't be any.
> It follows that the unpleasant is not tenable.
> (chapter XXIII, verse 10-11)[68]

His statement is quite clear. One cannot know the experience of pleasure (or displeasure) without also, and at the same time, invoking its polar opposite. Therefore, it can be said that they exist independently, in the conventional sense, but they cannot individually possess inherent (independent) existence in the ultimate sense. The pairs of opposites contained within any concept are intimately tied to one another and depend upon each other for their own existence.

It is important to realize that this refers to *any* mental conception that could be generated within the mind. Once I posit the existence of any object, I am immediately faced with some form of polar opposite which, at the very least, confirms the existence of my 'self' as a positing entity. Therefore, all mental conceptions are naturally dualistic because they stand juxtaposed against myself (i.e., a conceiving entity), and neither of the poles, in essence, are inherently existent.

The foundation for Nāgārjuna's position against thinking dualistically rests heavily upon a central logical argument that is employed throughout his text. The *catuskoti*, better known as the *tetralemma* or the Four Alternative Positions, was a fourfold method of logic used widely by the Mādhyamaka masters "solely for the purpose of awakening people to the truth of emptiness."[69] The clearest definition of the Tetralemma comes to us through the words of G. M. Nagao:

> The dialectic of Nāgārjuna is formulated in various ways, the most well-known being the tetralemma: being, non-being, both being and non-being, neither being nor non-being, a formulation meant to include all possible cases. Through analysis and critique of these four possibilities, all positions are revealed to be inherently contradictory insofar as they are formulated in a context of essences. The

deconstructive (*prāsaṅgika*) reasoning points to the emptiness of beings.[70]

Nāgārjuna relies upon the contradiction of antinomy. That is, a contradiction will arise between two equally binding laws or logical conclusions wherever notions of a self-existent independent nature is asserted. Nāgārjuna institutes this argument from the outset and demonstrates the illogic of dualistic thinking early into his project. In the first verse of his first chapter, entitled "Examination of Conditions," Nāgārjuna takes direct aim at the notions of causation which rely upon inherent existence.

> Neither from itself nor from another,
> Nor from both,
> Nor without a cause,
> Does anything whatsoever, anywhere arise.
> (chapter I, verse 1)[71]

Kalupahana notes that Nāgārjuna does not deny the empirical dependent-arising of phenomena; only their metaphysical independent existence.[72] This is a bold statement to begin Nāgārjuna's enquiry and it sets the pace for his subsequent arguments. As Garfield observes, "Nāgārjuna begins by stating the conclusion (I:1): Entities are neither self-caused nor do they come to be through the power of other entities."[73] We can follow this argument by looking at each of the four individual positions (constituting the Tetralemma) described in the verse. Each position represents "the relation between an active cause and its effect"[74] in terms of "powers as essential properties of substantially real causes."[75] Nāgārjuna's goal is to undermine all four positions at once and illustrate as clearly as possible that dualistic thinking, itself, is logically incoherent.

The first causal position holds that "all causation is really self-causation. A proponent of this view would argue that for a cause to be genuinely the cause of an effect, that effect must exist potentially in the cause."[76] The effect must exist *in potentio* in its cause and, once manifest, would be self-caused. Garfield invokes the example of the seed and the sprout to explain this in simpler terms. The sprout exists as a potential within the seed and, upon actualization, the sprout would be said to be self-caused. In order to upset the notion of an inherently existing phenomenon, Nāgārjuna examines the notion of the causal power for that phenomenon. Rather than closing the explanation loop for causal theories, the question of causal power itself is seen to create a fundamental contradiction:

> If there were a causal power, it itself, as a phenomenon, would either have to have conditions or not. If the former, there is a vicious explanatory regress, for then one has to explain how the powers to act are themselves brought about by the conditions, and this is the very link that is presupposed by the friends of powers to be inexplicable. One could posit powers the conditions have to bring about powers and powers the powers have to bring about effects. But this just moves one step further down the regress.
> If, on the other hand, one suggests that the powers have no condition, one is stuck positing uncaused and inexplicable occult identities as the explanans of causation.[77]

As Garfield has described above, Nāgārjuna is demonstrating that all causal activity depends upon conditions for the ceasing and arising of phenomena. This is the obvious step for Nāgārjuna to take in order to associate phenomena with conventional truth. To suggest that causation is dependent upon further conditions renders it essence-less and powerless. As Garfield confirms, "to regard something as without essence and without power is to regard it as merely conventional existence."[78] All phenomena, which are described as phenomena in the conventional sense, are conditionally existent (i.e. dependently arising):

> If one views phenomena as having and as emerging from causal powers, one views them as having essences and as being connected to the essences of other phenomena. This...is ultimately incoherent since it forces one at the same time to assert the *inherent existence* of these things, in virtue of their essential identity, and to assert their *dependence* and *productive* character, in virtue of the causal history and power. But such dependence and rational character...is incompatible with their inherent existence.[79]

To ascribe inherent existence to anything is to assert that it exists independently. This causes problems for adherents of the second position who claim that an inherently existent phenomenon is caused by another object or source. As Garfield reiterates, inherently existent independent entities "need no conditions for their production. Indeed, they could not be produced if they exist in this way."[80]

To be produced is to be produced by either itself or by another. If by another, then it cannot be inherently existent. If produced by itself then, as we have shown, that causal power is itself a phenomenon which requires explanation. One is forced, once again, into an infinite regress of causes and causal conditions.

The third condition identified by the Tetralemma is that a thing is caused both by self *and* from another. This third argument amounts to little more than self-contradiction. As we saw in the first argument, an object that is self-caused is independent of the need for other causes or conditions. It is incoherent to suggest that an inherently existent entity is self-caused yet depends also on causation from another. This contradicts the notion of inherent existence from the outset.

Finally, the fourth position, that an inherently existent object is neither self-caused nor caused by another, suffers an even worse fate of contradiction than the previous proposition. This is tantamount to the assertion that things simply exist from no particular cause. In essence, they are not caused but have existed always. We would also be faced with the idea here that inherently existent entities are unchanging and static in their state of eternal existence – that is, the entity would necessarily eternally exist without change.

So these four arguments or positions provide a powerful weapon against the claim for self-existence and self-existent independent objects, as well as against the notion of dualistic thinking. All four positions contradict the claim that an object has a distinct essence or inherent existence. In fact, not only are the objects empty of essence, they are empty of causal powers. It is only due to this fact – that there are no *actual* inherent existences – that the doctrine of dependent arising (*pratītya-samutpāda*) can be asserted in the first place, because an inherent existence could never arise but would be eternally-existing, without change. It is through the doctrine of dependent arising (*pratītya-samutpāda*) that *process* can be asserted. Furthermore, Nāgārjuna's statement on emptiness (e.g., that all things are empty of inherent existence) can be used to describe not only the phenomena themselves but also their causes. As Garfield explains:

> Effects lacking inherent existence depend precisely upon conditions that themselves lack inherent existence.... To say that causation is nonempty, or inherently existent, is to succumb to the temptation to ground our explanatory practice and discourse in genuine causal powers linking causes to effects. That is the reificationist extreme that Nāgārjuna clearly rejects. To respond to the arguments against the inherent existence of causation by suggesting that there is then no possibility of appealing to conditions to explain phenomena – that there is no dependent origination at all – is the extreme of nihilism, also clearly rejected by Nāgārjuna. To assert the emptiness of causation is to accept the utility of our causal discourse and explanatory practice, but to resist the temptation to see these as grounded in reference to causal powers or as demanding such grounding. Dependent origination simply is the explicability and coherence of the universe. Its emptiness is the fact that there is no more to it than that.[81]

The depth and importance of this last statement should not be underrated. It contradicts our dualistic experience of reality yet brings together the whole of Buddhist philosophy and practice into one consistent and logical nondual picture. The Tetralemma serves as Nāgārjuna's absolute defence against dualistic thinking as well as against any claims for inherent existence. So effective is this logical formula that he employs it throughout the text in both its negative and positive format.

It is important to note that each form of the tetralemma, negative or positive, is valid depending upon which view of the world – ultimate or conventional – one is speaking of. However, as noted at the outset of chapter 1, any *linguistic* interpretation of reality, according to Nāgārjuna, was only possible from the conventional point of view if one was to avoid sounding nonsensical.

Nagao emphasizes the necessity of Nāgārjuna's dialectical negation when discussing ultimate truth or inherent existence. If we assert existence in the positive sense we are apt to view it as substantial existence. This would result in a mistaken view of things:

> It is noted here that such a problem arises only from the views adhering to the idea of substantiality (*sasvabhāva-vāda*), not from those faithful to the idea of non-substantiality (*nihsvabhāva-vāda*). It is because the Tathāgata is believed to exist in this world substantively that it necessarily follows that he will cease to exist after death. The Tathāgata is 'Śūnya,' and questions regarding life after death is nonsense.[82]

The use of the negative form of the Tetralemma is necessary to avoid contradiction and inconsistency. "One can evade all of these paradoxes by simply rejecting the language of existence and nonexistence when these are read inherently. Empty things exist conventionally; but about their ultimate status, nothing can be literally said."[83]

The illogical position of dualist thinking is one of the key demonstrations underlying the entirety of Nāgārjuna's work. His usual approach is through the method of negation and the formula that is often applied is the negative form of the Tetralemma. He makes plain that the dualistic approach of asserting essential or inherent existence to objects or conditions in the world has both illogical and incoherent outcomes. Furthermore, he illustrates the fact that one cannot assert anything about existence other than that it is empty and that that emptiness, likewise, is itself empty of inherent existence.

The illogic of dualist thinking, along with the Tetralemma and the emptiness of conventional truth, has provided the groundwork for my subsequent analysis of Nāgārjuna's text in the light of the remaining four nondual categories. It will become apparent that the four remaining categories of nondualism can only advance under the strength and coherence of this first category. For this reason, Nāgārjuna seems to have established this first type of essential nonduality early in his project.

Nonduality – The Nonplurality of the World

It is widely acknowledged that Nāgārjuna was not the originator of nondualist philosophy. However, it might be argued that he was, perhaps, one of its most thorough defenders. In the previous chapter, I showed that Nāgārjuna's 'middlest' stance exploited the Tetralemma early on as a method to validate the illogical position of dualist thinking. This step allowed him to elaborate upon subsequent forms of nondualism. If, as Nāgārjuna has shown, it is inconsistent to speak of inherent (individual) existence then it follows naturally that the world of phenomena is fundamentally nonplural. From this position, phenomena are considered as attributes, properties, characteristics, or appearances of the one nondual whole. As Loy contends, this can be inferred "because all the things 'in' the world are not really distinct from each other but together constitute some integral whole."[84] In fact, a powerful relationship exists between this aspect of nondualism and the one described in the previous chapter. This is due to the fact that "dualistic conceptual thinking is what causes us to experience a pluralistic world."[85]

Many terms have been used to refer to this notion of a nonplural whole. Across the spectrum of Eastern philosophical traditions we encounter such terms as the *Tao, Ātman/Brahman, Dharmakāya, Dharmadhātu, Tathatā,* the Absolute, and the One Mind. A description of their qualities is more often identified by what they are not, rather than what they are, and they are often described in the various texts by terms such as 'colorless,' 'odourless,' 'formless,' or 'without appearance.'[86] Yet, even this negative attempt at description is somewhat dualistic and suffers the same incoherence, to some extent, as was elaborated upon in the previous chapter. For Nāgārjuna, one can only emphasize the emptiness (*śūnya*) of all appearances. To speak of it as inherently existing is simply misleading. As Loy reiterates, "any Tao that can be Tao'd is not the real Tao,"[87] and this statement certainly applies as a metaphor for Nāgārjuna's notion of emptiness, although the two are not directly comparable in all respects. It also speaks to the difficulty raised earlier in defining nondualism.

The rudimentary habit of thinking pluralistically begins with the notion of the *relations* that appear to exist between the appearances or forms. This is exactly what Nāgārjuna challenges in his treatise with a mechanism called the *fivefold analysis*. The fivefold analysis examines the conception of the relationship *itself* between any subject (i.e., the notion of any inherently existent self) and its features or properties (i.e., the aggregates). It involves the examination of five *possible* relations that might exist between objects and their properties or characteristics. These five possible relations are, 1) that the object and its properties are identical, 2) that the object and its properties are independent or distinct from one another, 3) that the object stands outside of its properties yet exists as a basis for them, 4) that the object is contained in the aggregates or properties, and 5) that the object is distinct from, yet dependent upon, the properties.[88]

An example of the fivefold analysis can be found in Nāgārjuna's 23rd chapter on the "Examination of Errors." In this chapter he scrutinizes the relationship between the individual and its defilements or impurities.

> The defilements are somebody's.
> But that one has not been established.

> Without the possessor,
> The defilements are nobody's.
>
> View the defilements as you view yourself:
> They are not in the defiled in the fivefold way.
> View the defiled as you view your self:
> It is not in the defilements in the fivefold way.
> (chapter XXIII, verse 4, 5)[89]

In this section of the text, Nāgārjuna is denying the inherent existence of defilements (although we could substitute any human attribute here) on the basis that it is illogical to posit any *actual* relationship between the defilement and its possessor. Based upon the fivefold analysis, Nāgārjuna is adamant about denying that any relationship can be spoken of as existing between the defiled and the defilements (i.e., between a subject and its attributes). The belief in a plurality of inherently existent characteristics is illogical on the grounds that it is incoherent to assert the existence of a relationship to oneself of a quality that one already *is*.

This is described in a previous chapter dealing with the "Examination of the Tathāgata." In that chapter, Nāgārjuna analyzes the specific relations between the self and the aggregates. He invokes the symbol of the Buddha's self but, as Garfield affirms, "the analysis is perfectly general as a refutation of any assertion of an inherently existent personal self."[90]

> Neither the aggregates, nor different from the aggregates,
> The aggregates are not in him, nor is he in the aggregates.
> The Tathāgata does not possess the aggregates.
> What is the Tathāgata?

> If the Buddha depended on the aggregates,
> He would not exist through an essence.
> Not existing through an essence,
> How could he exist through otherness-essence?
> (chapter XXII, verse 1, 2)[91]

Following this statement, Nāgārjuna then presents the five possible relations for analysis and goes on, in subsequent verses, to question the coherence of each relation in turn. By undermining each form of relation, Nāgārjuna establishes grounds for the nonplurality of the world.

Garfield describes two reasons that Nāgārjuna offers on why the first type of relation – that the self cannot be identical with the aggregates – is incoherent. "First, the self posited is meant to be unitary, and the aggregates are plural. Second, the aggregates are constantly undergoing change, while the self that is posited is meant to endure as a single entity."[92] This first type of relation suggests contradictory states between the inherently existent self, which is permanent and unchanging, and the aggregates, which are always changing. Therefore, this disparity between the notions of permanence and impermanence rules out the first relation of identity through self-contradiction.

The second type of relation – that the self and the aggregates are different – falls on an alternative contradiction. That is, "anything that happens to the aggregates happens to the self, and vice versa."[93] In effect, for example, if an injury occurs to an individual's aggregates, it necessarily injures *that person*. Therefore, it makes no sense to suggest a relation, and therefore a distinction, between the self and the aggregates. Garfield makes a further point regarding this particular form of relation: "buddhahood is presumably attained by a purification of the aggregates through practice. If the aggregates were entirely different from the self, it is not clear how purifying *them* would lead the *practitioner* to buddhahood."[94] Indeed, what would be the use of any modification to the aggregates? This form of relation, as a result, must also be rejected.

The third form of relation is easier to deconstruct than the previous two. Nāgārjuna posits the typical Vedāntic view that the self might stand outside the aggregates as a basis for them. Likewise, he offers the alternative to this position in the fourth possible relation – that the self is contained in the aggregates. Both of these views are defeated by mentally subtracting either one or the other from the equation. In doing so, he removes the last remaining positions that might support the notion of an inherent existence for the self.

> The self cannot stand outside the aggregates as a basis for them, for if we strip away all of the aggregates, there is nothing left as an independent support. But nor is the self somehow contained in the aggregates as a hidden core, and for the same reason. When we strip away all of the aggregates in thought, nothing remains of the self.[95]

The third and fourth types of relation are eradicated when we attempt to identify one aspect of the polarity as distinct and inherently existent without the other. This leaves us with only one relation left to examine.

The fifth category of relation is examined as the possibility that "the self . . . is distinct from but dependent upon the aggregates."[96] This is an obscure form of relation, yet it fails to pass the rigorous examinations by Nāgārjuna. As Kalupahana explains, this is a denial by Nāgārjuna of some of the Substantialist's positions which allowed for the existence of a 'freed' or enlightened individual who no longer was dependent upon the aggregates, yet who still retain them for use. According to Kalupahana, it was argued that such a freed person might continue to 'cling' to the aggregates without being dependent upon them like persons still in bondage.[97] Furthermore, it is in response to this position that Nāgārjuna is disputing "that if a *tathāgata* (an enlightened Buddha) were to exist without grasping onto the aggregates (*skandhān anupādāya*), he will still be dependent upon (*upādayād*) them at the present time (*idānīm*), that is, as long as he is alive."[98]

Garfield holds much the same view and, if one comes to think of the Buddha as a freed person with inherent existence, this possible relation becomes nonsensical:

> For if the Buddha were dependent, he would lack an essence and would be empty. And the situation can't be saved by suggesting that he has an essence through a relation to another since that presupposes essential difference, which presupposes that both the Buddha and the aggregates on which he is supposed to depend have individual essences.[99]

Any indication of dependence upon another for existence undermines the Substantialist's position. By suggesting that the Buddha, despite being 'freed,' is still dependent in any way upon the aggregates contradicts the notion of 'freedom' in the first place. This last type of relation is then rejected along with the previous four.

From this standpoint, the five possible types of relation are not coherent in relation to the Substantialist's position of inherent existence. This is a key point. If it is incoherent or contradictory to speak of relations at all then we will have no alternative but to admit the nonplurality of the world. The belief in plurality depends largely upon the belief that relations exist between objects which are deemed to be distinct and separate from each other. By undermining the notion of relations, Nāgārjuna has also called into question the existence of plurality. Despite the appearances that exist in the world, it must be thought of in nonpluralistic terms as long as the notion of relations remains incoherent.

A clearer picture of Nāgārjuna's position will ensue by looking at similar arguments made by F. H. Bradley. This logician and metaphysician of the 20th century used a system of reasoning and logic, analogous to that of Nāgārjuna, to undermine the notion of relations and, consequently, plurality. Richard Wolheim summarizes Bradley's approach regarding reality.

> The first and most important single doctrine contained in the [Bradley's] system is that Reality is One: that though to all appearance there may be in the world many different things -- tables, chairs, grains of sand, the animals in the zoo, the fishes in the ocean, leaves in the wind -- all of which are discrete and diverse, in truth there is only one vast thing, the World. In support of this view, Bradley argues in two different ways: first, from the impossibility of many reals, secondly, from the notion of Substance.[100]

Bradley's nondualist position is best understood in the context of his first argument – the impossibility of many 'reals' – which requires an understanding of the notions of *internal* and *external* relations. Internal relations are those relations to attributes or characteristics that are necessary to define an object's existence. For example, an internal relation of a bachelor is in being an 'unmarried man.' Without that relation, he could not be a bachelor. An external relation, on the other hand, is that this same bachelor lives in an apartment. By its absence or presence, the bachelor still retains his 'bachelor-ness.'

The notion of pluralism, which Bradley takes aim at defeating, maintains that reality contains self-subsistent entities or, what Bradley calls 'independent reals' (this is akin to Nāgārjuna's notion of inherently existent entities). Bradley points out that the qualities of any object must both support their relations as well as be defined by their relations. "Each has a double character, as both supporting and as being made by a relation."[101] Each relation between independent reals, therefore, must be both internal and external, at the same time, and for each real. This produces a contradiction and creates a problem for the concept of plurality. Wollheim gives us an explanation of this:

> Let us take two independent reals, X and Y, and the relation that holds between them – for since they are [apparently] two, there must be a relation holding between them. Now, regarded from the point of view of X, the relation that X has to Y ought to be internal to X: for if X is to be independent, then the properties that it possesses (and that includes relational properties) must arise from its nature not from some external cause. But, of course, from the point of view of Y and

its independence, this would be fatal. For if the relation of X to Y were internal to X, then Y would in part at least be dependent on the nature of X. In other words,...every real demands that every relation that it has with every other real be internal to it and external to the other real; and such a demand, when fully generalized, is, of course, self-contradictory.[102]

Accordingly, pluralism is a logically impossible assertion because of the incoherence of speaking in terms of relations. Nāgārjuna's position is clearly substantiated by Bradley's assertions. As Wollheim contends, Bradley's unapologetic view endorses the position that, epistemologically speaking, "the apparent externality of some relations, like the apparent contingence of some judgments, [are] merely the projection of our ignorance upon the world."[103] Similar to Nāgārjuna's estimation, we adhere to the belief in relations as a result of our mistaken interpretation of reality.

The description by Bradley gives us further insight into this portion of Nāgārjuna's argument. As each has shown, it is incoherent to speak of relations in terms of inherent existence (i.e., as one of Bradley's 'reals'). The concept of plurality remains just that – a mental concept, or epistemological perspective – and exists as a reflection of the way the objects appear and arise via sensory contact with the world. This is the crux of dependent origination and it is only *because* of Nāgārjuna's claim – that relations are illogical and illusory – that there follow any grounds for dependent origination (*pratītya-samutpāda*). As Tola and Dragonetti point out, "*Pratītyasamutpāda* literally means 'dependent origination,' but in the arena of the Mādhyamika school it can be translated by 'Universal Relativity', as

Stcherbatsky rightly does."[104] Mansfield, however, wades in to this debate with an important qualification of the term 'relativity':

> In the Maadhyamika translations and commentaries the fundamental philosophic use of relativity is dependency, interconnectedness, and relation to a knower. However, in modern physics, this is only the smaller part of its meaning. The physical principle of relativity more fundamentally embodies the independence of a particular observer, universality, and a degree of absoluteness – completely antithetical to the use of relativity in Maadhyamika. Conflating these divergent meanings of the term relativity can lead to confusion and a misunderstanding of the doctrine of emptiness.[105]

Therefore, the notion of *dependent origination*, in Mādhyamaka, can be used to account for the relative appearance of distinct phenomena instead of having to rely upon the notion of inherent existence for phenomena. This should not be confused with the idea of relativity in classical physics which might allow for such an inherent existence. According to Nāgārjuna, the plurality of the world is conventionally real but ultimately empty (*śūnya*).

It is clear from this analysis that Nāgārjuna has utilized this 3rd aspect of nondualism to point to the illusory nature of relationship and relations. This results in an affirmation of the nonplurality of the world and distinct phenomena. Having identified this aspect of nondualist thinking within the *Mūlamadhyamakakārikā* a foundation is now set for the next aspect of nondualism. This next category – *the nondifference of subject and object* – brings the view of nondualism closer to home. As a consequence of Nāgārjuna's dialectical reasoning, individuals must now question their own inherent existence and independence.

Nonduality – The Nondifference of Subject and Object

This third approach to nonduality is often one of the most counterintuitive of the five categories for individuals to grasp. In the ultimate sense, individual subjects simply do not exist. According to Nāgārjuna's claims, the individual's belief in the reality of 'self,' as an inherently existing entity, is mistaken. However, in terms of conventional reality, the complex of feelings, emotions, thoughts, and physical attributes come together realistically to form an empirical – albeit, transitory – existence. Within the realm of conventional truth, this aggregate of properties (characteristics) comprise the sum total of any given identity for the human being and generate – *within this identity itself* – a belief in its own inherent and autonomous existence.

Nāgārjuna's philosophical position would suggest that these properties are empty of inherent existence. Further, the identity, which is accepted by that subjective being as something real, is empty and subsists only as a temporary manifestation arising dependently under the cyclic activity portrayed in the notion of *pratītya-samutpāda*. Professor Susumu Yamaguchi, of Ōtani University in Kyoto, Japan, states:

> Our daily life is functional upon the basis of our conceptivally differentiated outlook, considering that there is *'one who speaks'* and *'words spoken'* as well as a *'knower'* and *'things to be known'*—in this manner our world of ignorant suffering manifests itself. At the very foundation of this situation we can perceive our mind attempting to grasp or cognize (*upalabdhi*) objectivity in the form of a substance having the nature of an entity. And the

> fact that we possess such a mind that attempts to grasp a substantial entity is the basic cause of our suffering.[106]

Yamaguchi is here referring to the tendencies within individuals to reify objective phenomena and, like Nāgārjuna, he feels that it is at the core of suffering for the individual.

This third conceptualization of nondualism relies upon the use of negation to establish its point. Various philosophical positions typically negate the duality of subject-object by collapsing one of the poles of the opposites (subject/object) into the other. The early Buddhist doctrine of *Anātman* usually collapses the subject into the object so that, in all existence, there is only the Absolute. The individual self, or *Ātman*, is merely an *appearance* of the Absolute. The main Buddhist injunction is for the individual to avoid mistaking the appearances for the reality.

> Those who think the unreal is, and think the Real is not, they shall never reach the Truth, lost in the path of right thought.
>
> But those who know the Real is, and know the unreal is not, they shall indeed reach the Truth, safe on the path of right thought.
> (*The Dhammapada*, chapter 1, verses 9-12)[107]

The important aspect of this passage is that the appearance of objects in the world creates a false impression about reality.

Advaita Vedānta, while expressing nondualism in its own way, often takes the opposite turn and collapses the object into the subject. According to this view, emphasis is placed on *Ātman*. There is only *Ātman* and all things reside in the Self. At other times, it seems as though it is also prepared to de-objectify the *Ātman*. Nevertheless, its center of attention remains focused on the notion of *Ātman*. As mentioned earlier, this is likely due to the fact that much that is written in the Eastern philosophical tradition is concerned with the release and liberation of the individual. This model is evident within the Upanishadic tradition:

> For when there is a duality of some kind, then the one can smell the other, the one can see the other, the one can hear the other, and the one can perceive the other. When, however, the Whole has become one's very self (*ātman*), then who is there for one to smell and by what means? (Brhadāranyaka Upanisad II.iv.14)[108]

This same idea is later expressed in a more direct fashion:

> About this self (*ātman*), one can only say 'not —, not ——.' He is ungraspable, for he cannot be grasped. He is undecaying, for he is not subject to decay.... A man who knows this, therefore, becomes calm, composed, cool, patient, and collected. He sees the self (*ātman*) in just himself (*ātman*) and all things as the self. (Brhadāranyaka Upanisad IV.iv.22, 23)[109]

This Vedāntic perspective looks to the Self, the *Ātman*, for the achievement within the individual's experience of universality and oneness. Although Nāgārjuna uses a different approach, he develops the same aspect of nondualism in his dialectical process by dissolving the distinctions between the self and the world.

It is important to his project that Nāgārjuna resist collapsing one end of the dualistic framework into the other. This is what partially distinguishes his position from both the earlier Buddhist movement, which collapses the self into the Absolute, and Advaita Vedāntic movement which, in many instances, collapses objective reality into the Self. Instead, he must show that both poles – the subject *and* the object – are empty and exist only in the conventional sense.

The process of dismantling the dualist's subject-object view does not occur in any one place. Rather, Nāgārjuna takes successive elements of the dualist claims throughout the text and deconstructs each one according to the doctrine of emptiness. It is this process which is of concern to us in this chapter.

For the sake of understanding the progression of Nāgārjuna's argument, Garfield artificially divides the *Mūlamadhyamakakārikā* into four main stages of argument with progressively complex concepts.[110] According to these stages, Garfield shows how Nāgārjuna utilizes his dialectical method to progressively dismantle the arguments put forth by the various schools of detractors and critics. The dialectic of the first seven chapters is set up to examine some of the "fundamental theoretical constructs of Buddhist ontology, such as dependent origination, change and impermanence, perception, the aggregates that compose the self, the elements that constitute the universe, and the relation between substance and attribute."[111] This allows Nāgārjuna to establish certain parameters regarding causation and existence according to both conventional and ultimate truth.

One essential theme that emerges in this first stage is that "a wide range of phenomena, including external perceptibles, psychological processes, relations, putative substances, and attributes...are empty."[112] That is, these phenomena are void of any inherent existence according to ultimate truth, but do exist dependently within conventional truth.

These are important observations and provide the background for his subsequent dialectic. The next stage, suggested by Garfield, stretches from chapter VIII to XIII. In this section, "Nāgārjuna focuses on the nature of the self and of subjective experience."[113]

> An existent entity has no activity.
> There would also be action without an agent.
> An existent entity has no activity.
> There would also be agent without action.
> (chapter VIII, verse 2)[114]

This is Nāgārjuna's first major attack to the subject side of the subject-object polarity. The difficulty that Nāgārjuna must overcome is in dealing with the idealist assertion that while the samsaric (illusory) world may be a mistaken view, there must still necessarily exist a subject who *has* that mistaken view. To do this, Nāgārjuna examines the qualities that a subject possesses and the relationship between the subject and predicate. For example, in questions pertaining to action one must determine whether one's actions are separate from oneself or whether the actions *are* oneself.

In any attempt to determine the subject as inherently existent, a detractor would be forced to describe action as if it were separate from the agent so that at one moment the agent might exhibit action and at another moment be devoid of action. We make reference to the agent or to the action as if they were distinct topics for consideration or discussion. If we do this, however, we run into some logical problems:

> If the agent were inherently existent, then it would be unchanging. Activity is always a kind of change. So if there were action in the context of an inherently existing agent, the action would be agentless, which would be absurd. Moreover, the agent would be inactive, which would also be absurd. This, of course, is just one more case of Nāgārjuna demonstrating the incoherence of a position that tries both to posit inherently existent, independent entities and then to get them to interact.[115]

It is this conceptual fragmentation, between agent and action, which brings incoherence to the arguments for inherent existence. If some agent can be said to be inherently existent and independent of its actions then one must also be prepared to accept the fact of an actionless agent as well as an agentless action. This, of course, would be an irrational statement. For Nāgārjuna:

> Someone is disclosed by something.
> Something is disclosed by someone.
> Without something how can someone exist?
> Without someone how can something exist?
> (chapter IX, verse 5)[116]

The central emphasis in Nāgārjuna's assertion is on the "correlativity and interdependence of subject and object.

Subjectivity only emerges when there is an object of awareness. Pure subjectivity is a contradiction *in adjecto*."[117] In other words, the self cannot exist at all other than as an entity that dependently arises through an action or any other predicate.

Additionally, it is important to add a note of qualification by pointing out that Nāgārjuna is not claiming an identity between the action and agent. Rather, that both are empty and interdependent.

Finally, it should be remembered that it is the interdependent (but empty) aggregate of qualities that constitute the empty subject, which conceives itself as inherently existent. This *conceived-of-as-inherently-existent-self* continues to appropriate qualities that supplement and enhance its own illusory self-conception.

It is tempting, at this stage of the argument, to continue to fall back into restoring the belief that one can witness or perceive this *conceived-of-as-inherently-existent-self* as an illusion while, at the same time, continuing to subtly believe in one's own inherent existence or substantiality. By recognizing this habitual reifying reflex, the individual will be able to identify the illusory *conceived-of-as-inherently-existing-self* witnessing its own *conceived-of-as-inherently-existing-self*. This is a vicious regress that traps the individualized consciousness and demonstrates the seemingly innate drive to assert and re-assert one's own independent existence despite the obvious evidence to the contrary.

In recognizing this process of reification one can come to see the necessity of practices such as reflection upon Zen koans or Buddhist forms of meditation that serve to overcome the mind's self-affirming activities. As Garfield observes, "the self that is constructed through appropriation presents itself as the subject of appropriation. But it is merely constructed, and its substantial reality is illusory."[118]

Therefore, Nāgārjuna has succeeded in negating the inherent existence of the subject and, further, he argues that a substantial entity cannot somehow exist apart from its qualities and actions. The self only exists as a dependently arising phenomenon in relation to its qualities and actions. "In all cases of the relation between an agent of any kind and an act of any kind, the identity of the two will be seen to be mutually dependent, and each will come out as conventionally real, though not as inherently existent."[119] This supports the idea of co-dependent origination and is a significant part of Nāgārjuna's argument throughout the entire book. His negation of an inherently existent subject fulfills half of the conditions for this aspect of nondualism. What remains for him is to develop an argument that negates the inherent existence of the object.

Continuing the analysis within the stages set out by Garfield, the third part of the *Mūlamadhyamakakārikā* consists of chapters XIV to XXI. These chapters are "primarily concerned with the external world and relation of the self to objects."[120] This is a crucial component of Nāgārjuna's dialectic. Previously, he has examined the basic ontological principles in Buddhist philosophy and found them to be empty of inherent existence in the ultimate sense. His subsequent analysis of the subjective self and its qualities and predicates has likewise found them to be ultimately empty, yet conventionally real and interdependent. The strategy he employs in this section of the text examines notions of the connection between components in compounded phenomena, essence, bondage to cyclic existence, the effects of actions, and the nature of self and time. His dialectic, once again, reveals the lack of inherent existence in any of these concepts.

For our purposes, however, the most valuable section is chapter XV – "Examination of Essence." It is here that Nāgārjuna provides the final stage of the argument required to substantiate this third category of nondualism. As Garfield explains of this chapter:

> Nāgārjuna rejects the coherence of the concept of essence and explores its ramifications for the concept of inherent existence, the concept of an entity, and the concept of a nonentity. This chapter is also aimed at dispelling any nihilistic interpretation of the Mādhyamika philosophical orientation and in explaining the deep connection between the analysis of phenomena as empty of essence and the demonstration of the possibility of empirical reality.[121]

By focusing on essence, Nāgārjuna is undermining the characteristic by which phenomena are claimed to be inherently real. "For when Nāgārjuna argues that phenomena are all empty, it is *of* essence in this sense that they are empty."[122] The argument used against the inherent existence of essence is similar to the method he has employed throughout, and its conclusions are just as obvious.

> Without having essence or otherness-essence,
> How can there be entities?

> If there are essences and entities
> Entities are [already] established.
> (chapter XV, verse 4)[123]

As seen earlier, Nāgārjuna illustrates the emptiness of phenomena by demonstrating the incoherence of inherently existent essences. "The concept of an inherently existent entity is the concept of an entity with an essence. So without essence, there are no inherently existing entities."[124] Phenomena (i.e., objects) are empty and dependent upon causes and conditions (i.e., subjects) for their conventional existence. Further, the relationships between subjects and objects are also empty of inherent existence and they arise dependently as characteristics of phenomena. He can now make the claim that objects, likewise, are empty and this final point establishes the nondifference of subject and object. They are both empty of inherent existence and only arise as properties or conditions in one universal whole.

It is clear that this third aspect of nondualism – *the nondifference of subject and object* – exists as a consequence of the several arguments made throughout the text. This is a much larger position for Nāgārjuna to argue, for it encompasses more complex themes than are found in the earlier stages of his dialectic. Subsequently, it should not be surprising that it arises out of a combination and consequence of the earlier two categories.

In relation to Nāgārjuna's project, however, this stage is not the end and there remains a further step to be taken. He does this in the final section of the *Mūlamadhyamakakārikā*, from chapter XXII to XXVII, and this leads us to our fourth aspect of nondualism – *the identity of phenomenon and the Absolute*.

Nonduality – The Identity of Phenomenon and the Absolute

This fourth category of nondualism, as with the others, arises out of the previous types and is really an amalgamation of the first three. The theme of this category is similar to the conclusion reached by Nāgārjuna in the last chapters of the *Mūlamadhyamakakārikā*. In this final stage of Garfield's fourfold division of the text (chapters XXII to XXVII) Nāgārjuna "addresses phenomena associated with the ultimate truth, such as buddhahood, emptiness, and nirvāna, and the relation of the conventional to the ultimate and of samara to nirvāna."[125]

As in previous chapters, these notions, too, will be found to be empty in the ultimate sense, yet empirically real and dependently arising in the conventional sense.

> Having passed into nirvāna, the Victorious Conqueror
> Is neither said to be existent
> Nor is said to be nonexistent.
> Neither both nor neither are said.
>
> So, when this victorious one abides, he
> Is neither said to be existent
> Nor said to be nonexistent.
> Neither both nor neither are said.
>
> There is not the slightest difference
> Between cyclic existence [samsāra] and nirvāna.
> There is not even the slightest difference
> Between nirvāna and cyclic existence.
>
> Whatever is the limit of nirvāna,
> That is the limit of cyclic existence.

> There is not even the slightest difference between them,
> Or even the subtlest thing.
> (chapter XXV, verse 17-20)[127]

Essentially, Nāgārjuna argues for the emptiness of emptiness itself. Loy refers to this as "the nonduality of duality and nonduality,"[126] and it represents the climaxing move in Nāgārjuna's dialectic.

This can be a startling and difficult conclusion to accept for one grounded in the dualist perspective. It undermines the ultimate existence of both samsāra and nirvāna and speaks directly to the nondifference between conventional truth and ultimate truth or, in terms of Nāgārjuna's arguments and, by extension, this fourth aspect of nondualism, *between phenomena and the Absolute*.

If Nāgārjuna intends to deconstruct all that can be known then he must also demonstrate the emptiness of nirvāna itself and even, ultimately, his own doctrine. As Loy suggests, a truly complete nondual system of thought must also deconstruct itself to make way for the "possibility for a new, nonconceptual 'opening' to something very different."[128] Furthermore, this ultimate self-deconstruction might lead "to a transformed mode of experiencing the world."[129]

This last point is crucial to understanding Nāgārjuna's undertaking. He is not asserting a positive ontological claim about reality. Instead, Nāgārjuna is pointing to the epistemological error that we are victim to in relation to our understanding and perception of reality.[130] In doing so, he is potentially opening the door to a new experience of reality. Nirvāna (or, in the West, the Kingdom of Heaven) is not a destination that one can seek out or move toward. In the ultimate sense, it is everywhere at all times and its realization only requires that we view reality-as-it-is. Therefore, when reality is perceived through a conditioned (dualist) perspective we call it samsāra. Alternatively, where reality is perceived through an unconditioned (nondual) perspective then it becomes ineffable, although we refer to that experience as nirvāna.

> There is only one reality – this world, right here and now – but this world may be experienced in two different ways. Samsāra is the relative, phenomenal world as usually experienced, which is delusively understood to consist of a collection of discrete objects (including 'me') that interact causally in space and time. Nirvāna is that same world but as it is in itself, nondually incorporating both subject and object into a whole.[131]

Nāgārjuna employs the negative Tetralemma once again to emphasize that he cannot refer to the notion of nirvāna in the ultimate sense. This is necessary, as Garfield explains, in order to avoid "talking nonsense" about the ultimate nature of things. All phenomena lack inherent existence and cannot be spoken of as existent in any substantial way. Instead, phenomena arise in relation to causes and conditions that are, in themselves, empty. Donald Lopez discusses this point further:

> Each phenomenon is empty of true existence and that mere absence of true existence is the final nature of the phenomenon. Dependent arising is, loosely speaking, the positive implication of the absence of true existence. All phenomena are dependent arisings in the sense that they either arise in dependence on causes and conditions, are designated in dependence on

their basis of imputation, or are imputed in dependence on a designating term or thought.¹³²

This leaves us in the awkward position of being unable to say anything *real* about the phenomenon. In fact, the Buddha sometimes employed silence as the expression of the truth about ultimate things. Nagao asserts that this silence, exhibited by the Buddha in relation to questions on nirvāna (or toward any metaphysical absolute, for that matter), was due to the ineffable nature of the ultimate metaphysical reality. "Even for the Saint, for whom the knowledge of the Absolute is accessible, it remains incommunicable; it remains silent forever. No doors of verbal designation or logic leads to the paramārtha."¹³³ It is worthy to note that Nagao borrows from the Yogācārin understanding of paramārtha as something 'unthinkable' (*acintya*), 'inexpressible' (*anabhilāpya*), and 'unconditioned' (*asamskrta*).¹³⁴

Yet, in a strange way, there seems to be a way in which one can be conscious of nirvāna, or to experience existence as it is, once consciousness has been deconditioned from the process of self-reification. This, after all, is defined clearly within the Four Noble Truths as the result of practicing the Eightfold Noble Path. While nirvāna remains ineffable, it nevertheless can be 'entered into' consciously and perceptually. The difficulty, it seems, is in overcoming dualist perspective and the tendency toward the reification of distinct subjects and objects. As Loy suggested earlier, it must occur through a "transformed mode" of experience¹³⁵ and seems to require a paradigm shift in the way we interpret reality.

Nonduality – The Identity of Phenomenon and the Absolute

Nāgārjuna attempts to give us a sense of the paradox that arises when trying to describe ultimate reality and shows, in the end, that it is an unthinkable and unknowable reality:

> That there is a self has been taught,
> And the doctrine of no-self,
> By the Buddhas, as well as the
> Doctrine of neither self nor nonself.
>
> What language expresses is nonexistent.
> The sphere of thought is nonexistent.
> Unarisen and unceased, like nirvāna
> Is the nature of things.
>
> Everything is real and not real.
> Both real and not real,
> Neither real nor not real.
> This is Lord Buddha's teaching
>
> Not dependent on another, peaceful and
> Not fabricated by mental fabrication,
> Not thought, without distinctions,
> That is the character of reality (that-ness).
> (chapter XVIII, verses 6-9)[136]

Garfield identifies an irony in the above passage in that all reality that is experienced by *conditioned* consciousness can only be experienced as *conventional* reality. Therefore, "seeing the conventional as conventional,...is to see it as it is ultimately."[137] It is in recognizing that all thoughts, feelings, appearances, and phenomena – including subjectivity itself – are empty. Garfield reiterates the fact that they are all dependently arising.

> Just as there is no difference in entity between the conventional and the ultimate, there is no

difference in entity between nirvāna and samsāra; nirvāna is simply samsāra seen without reification, without attachment, without delusion. The reason that we cannot say anything about nirvāna as an independent, nonsamsaric entity, then, is not that it *is* such an entity, but that it is ineffable and unknowable. Rather it is because it is only samsāra seen as it is, just as emptiness is just the conventional seen as it is.[138]

The difficulty encountered in *actually* overcoming the present dualistic paradigm in consciousness is in the interference produced by the individual's belief in a subjective self. Even while the notions presented by Nāgārjuna may come to be intellectually grasped, the individual will tend to subtly persist in the perspective that there is a very real 'I' that sees or understands this illusory notion. This reification of the "I" demonstrates, to some extent, the reflexive activity of the subjective self in approaching the topic *as* an enquirer. It is this attitude, *as* 'something,' which guarantees failure from the outset for anyone attempting to experience reality unconditionally.

This is clearly the central theme that Nāgārjuna has been developing and, by developing each of the previous themes of nondualism throughout his dialectical process, Nāgārjuna has come full circle. Not only are all phenomena empty but so too are Nāgārjuna's own concepts on emptiness. This must be so in order for his project to achieve a full nondualist metaphysic. In doing this he dissolves the apparent gap between conventional and ultimate truth, indicating further the nondifference between phenomenon and the Absolute. The perceived distinctions between the phenomenal world and the Absolute, according to Nāgārjuna's conclusions, are mistaken. Nāgārjuna has not 'located' the transcendent realm. Nor has he 'bridged' the phenomenal and the transcendent. Rather, he has argued that the Absolute *is* the phenomenal world and that the separation, far from existing in actuality, is merely the result of an epistemological error in our experience of reality. As Harris asserts, "neither nirvāna nor samsāra then are ontological terms."[139] It is from this mistaken epistemological interpretation of reality that samsaric existence – and its polar opposite, nirvāna – arise.

> To be in samsāra is to see things as they appear to deluded consciousness and to interact with them accordingly. To be in nirvāna, then, is to see those things as they are – as merely empty, dependent, impermanent, and nonsubstantial, but not to be somewhere else, seeing something else.... Nāgārjuna is emphasizing that nirvāna is not someplace else. It is a way of being here.[140]

This point has soteriological implications and is the basis for the fifth aspect of nondualism – *the possibility of a mystical union between the individual and the Absolute*. If there is no ultimate distinction to be made between the phenomenal world and the Absolute, other than what is required in order to overcome the epistemological errors, we may be able to forward the possibility of such a mystical union.

Nonduality – A Mystical Union Between the Individual and the Absolute

This fifth aspect of nondualism arises out of the implications of the first four categories and completes the list first described by David Loy. If Nāgārjuna has fulfilled the conditions of the first four aspects of nondualism – and it is clear that he has – then his work can be said to have important implications in relation to this last aspect. However, it is also critical to understand *in what fashion* Nāgārjuna might allow for that possibility of a mystical union between the individual and the Absolute.

Such a statement, at first glance, represents the same reificationist stance against which Nāgārjuna had argued from the start. It seems unlikely that this final aspect of nondualism can be related in any way to the arguments of the *Mūlamadhyamakakārikā*. To bridge this gap, we need to remember that Nāgārjuna's philosophical position is rooted in the 'two-truths' doctrine of reality. The point to be made in regards to this particular aspect of nondualism is that the notion of a mystical union between the individual and the Absolute naturally flows from the previous four aspects of nondualism and, further, that this notion naturally follows only within the *conventional* view of reality. From the arguments laid out by Nāgārjuna, this same claim would be fundamentally incoherent in the *ultimate* sense of reality.

To deal with this aspect of nondualism we need to go back to the fundamentals of the Two-Truths doctrine. Likewise, it would help us to understand in what sense a "seeker" must interact with that doctrine. Nagao provides an interesting insight in this regard:

> Religion is what begins from earnestly questioning, 'how is it that I exist?' or 'from whence do I come and to where do I go?' or 'for what purpose do I exist?'
>
> In that sense, religion has its beginnings when one's own existence is challenged with a great big question mark. This is not knowledge with regard to some object nor is it a concern that is outwardly directed. It is a question that comes from within with regard to one's own subjectivity.[141]

As Nagao here suggests, the desire to understand oneself and one's relationship to the world arises within the individual. At that moment, religion begins. The attempt to understand and define that fundamental relationship also serves to establish one's own identity. According to Nāgārjuna, this process of self-reification constitutes the links within the chain of dependent origination and gives eventual rise to the existence of the personality and a personal identity in the conventional sense. This 'grasping' for existence provides the conditioning by which the self-conceived individual, existent in the conventional sense, continues the reflexive process of reification.[142]

> Conditioned by feeling is craving.
> Craving arises because of feeling.
> When it appears, there is grasping,
> The four spheres of grasping.
>
> When there is grasping, the grasper
> Comes into existence.
> If he did not grasp,
> Then being freed, he would not come into existence.
> (chapter XXVI, verse 6, 7)[143]

Nonduality – A Mystical Union Between the Individual and the Absolute

The recognition of a reification process behind one's perspective of the world is a fundamental issue for Nāgārjuna and it has further soteriological implications. To move beyond this process of reification is to bring the individual nearer to release from samsāra.

The reification of phenomena, including the reification of a personal 'self,' dualistically conditions one's interpretive framework. As we saw earlier, the subjective self arises into *conventional existence* through appropriation, and later "presents itself as the subject of appropriation. But it is merely constructed, and its substantial reality is illusion."[144] It is not enough, however, to accept the temporary existence of a subjective self as a given. Regardless of how logical the argument might appear (i.e., that identity is somehow an impermanent illusion or that it is lacking in inherent existence) one's own personal identity still remains a very real experience for the individual.

This brings us back to Nagao's earlier comments. It is in the individual's experience of the first challenges to his or her existence, or the place of that existence in relation to the source of creation, that religion naturally arises. It is the search to relate to, and eventually unite with, the Absolute. This search finds its apex amongst the mystical traditions in both the East and West whose members often seek to resolve this fundamental sense of separation from the Absolute. The difficulty that confronts these individuals in ultimately fulfilling their search is that, according to the perspective offered in Nāgārjuna's dialectic, the dualistic categories of both the Absolute *and* the individual are empty. That is, neither the individual nor the Absolute exist *ultimately* but are present in awareness as conventional aspects of reality.

Both conceptions arise dependently, exist empirically in the *conventional* sense, and are sustained through the belief in a relationship between the two.

So, in relation to Nāgārjuna's *Mūlamadhyamakakārikā*, how can we speak of the possibility for a mystical union between the individual and the Absolute? Even the identification of oneself as a mystic would necessarily constitute a reification of identity and thus maintain one's conventional view of reality.

In his essay *"What Remains" in Śūnyatā*, Nagao analyzes the many well-known references to "what remains," which are usual terms employed to describe the resultant experience following enlightenment:

> Generally speaking, "what remains" is encountered by the practitioner when he is awakened; when consciousness is converted (*āśraya-parāvritti*) by training and becomes an entirely pure faith, the truth of tathāgatagarbha will be realized as "what remains." In the tathāgatagarbha doctrine, however, it is generally accepted that the tathāgatagarbha has always existed, so that it is actually not "what remains," but rather "what has existed from the beginning."[145]

The practitioner, through training, must move beyond the experiences of conventional truth to find "what remains." But conventional truth is not destroyed; it is only made *transparent*. Nagao speaks in the previous quote of the final conversion necessary to eventually understand the truth of *tathāgatagarbha*. The conversion spoken of comes about through the practitioner's own skill in overcoming and seeing beyond their dualistic conceptual framework. Nagao refers to this framework as *abhūtaparikalpa* – meaning "unreal notions" or "unreal imaginations" about the world – and speaks of these as the "actualities of life...which are a discrimination between, and attachment to, two things—the subject grasping and the object grasped (*grāhaka, grāhya*)."[146]

These "unreal imaginings" about the world are not removed from the practitioner's awareness entirely but, through training and conversion can become "pure and lucid."[147] This conceptual transparency, according to Nagao, can only occur due to the fact that they are empty to begin with. The conventional world becomes transparent through seeing the emptiness of the "unreal imaginations." Nagao relates that it is only "after śūnyatā is realized through *abhūtaparikalpa* [unreal imaginations], *abhūtaparikalpa* itself is re-realized as having always existed in 'emptiness' and as remaining forever, again in 'emptiness.'"[148] So the double structure in this notion of viewing the world must be known and understood by the practitioner in order to experience the ultimate transparency and emptiness of the dualistic perspective. As Nagao explains:

> With its double character of being and nonbeing, "emptiness" is the principle that underlies those old Mahāyānic sayings: "Defilement is identical with *bodhi*," "Birth and death are equal to nirvāna," "Without destroying defilements one enters into the nirvāna," and so on. The double structure found in the relationship between *abhūtaparikalpa* and śūnyatā represents the identity or the nonduality of samāra and nirvāna. Unless the double structure of the world, which is characterized as "empty," is apprehended, these

Mahāyānic sayings remain meaningless paradoxes.[149]

The solution to our question, therefore, arises directly from the implications of Nagao's explanation and, consistent with the method evidenced in Nāgārjuna's writings, materializes in the form of another negation. We can only posit the possibility of a mystical union by *first* understanding that the question itself is the result of a mistaken belief and can only be imagined from the *conventional* point of view. That is, the solution rests in the realization that *there is no inherent separation in the first place between the individual and the Absolute*. It is the individual's dualistic experience of reality that gives rise to notions of the individual and the Absolute and, likewise, it is through this duality that a perceived separation (or possible re-union between the two) arises.

The challenge, rather than seeking to unite with the Absolute, is to remove the veil of ignorance that prevents the individual's consciousness from experiencing reality-as-it-is. The perceived sense of separation, identified earlier as the foundation of conventional reality, is an epistemological error. It is the conventionally existing 'self,' mistakenly believing itself to be inherently existent in the ultimate sense, which longs for union with what is conceptualized as an inherently existent, and seemingly transcendent, Absolute. Maintaining this position gives rise to the belief in a relation between two inherently existing objects that must now somehow be bridged. It is this, and other mistakenly perceived relations, according to the Mādhyamika position, that causes suffering.

Nonduality – A Mystical Union Between the Individual and the Absolute

An individual, conditioned by the process of reification, grasps after that which is erroneously believed to be ultimately real. More than that, however, that individual desires that this *realness* apply first and foremost to its own identity.

> The Buddhist emphasis on the groundlessness of the ego-self implies that our most troublesome dualism is not life-versus-death but *being versus nothingness* (or *no-thing-ness*): the anxious self intuiting and dreading its own lack of being (or thing-ness). As a result, our sense-of-self is shadowed by a sense of *lack* that it perpetually yet vainly tries to resolve. The interdependence of bi-polar dualisms still holds: to the extent I come to feel autonomous, my consciousness is also infected with a gnawing sense of unreality, usually experienced as a vague feeling that 'there is something wrong with me.' Since we do not know how to cope with such an intimate sense of *lack*, it is repressed, only to return in projected form as the compulsive ways we attempt to make ourselves real in the world.[150]

As we have already seen, one form in which this conditioned behaviour unfolds (i.e., the conventional-self seeking existence in the ultimate sense) is through the search to unite with that ground of being (i.e. the Absolute) that is *already believed* to be inherently existent in the ultimate sense.

As recognized in traditional Buddhist beliefs, the experience of this compulsive need to reify oneself is one of suffering and, according to José Cabezón's interpretation of basic Buddhist convictions, this suffering can only cease when it is recognized that objects of perception "do not exist as they are apprehended by the mistaken conceptualization."[151] From Loy's point of view, this mistaken conceptualization, along with the resultant suffering, generates a basic experience of *lack*, which exacerbates the problem for the individual. Loy provides us with further insights into this line of reasoning:

> The ego-self's attempt to make itself real is a self-reflexive effort to grasp itself, an impossibility that leads to self-paralysis; Buddhist meditation, in which I become absorbed with my practice, is thus an exercise in deflection. To yield to my groundlessness is to realize that I have always been grounded: not as a sense-of-self, but insofar as I have never been separate from the world, never been other than the world.[152]

This statement approaches nearer to the position laid out by Nāgārjuna. Rather than attempting to answer directly to the possibility of a union between the individual and the Absolute, the individual must come to see that the 'desire to unite,' *itself*, can only arise dependently within a dualistic frame of mind grounded in a conventional view of reality. In recognizing the emptiness of such a view, one is left with the realization that the initial belief in an apparent separation between the individual and the Absolute was simply part of a mistaken view of reality.

The difficulty in comparing the notions of any mystical tradition to the arguments of Nāgārjuna, apart from the fact that there exists a wide range of interpretations for mysticism and the mystic's goal, is in the use of positive assertions. To put forward the positive existence of *any* inherent existence or ground of being, according to Nāgārjuna's position, simply creates another duality that must be negated, *ad infinitum*. Such an approach would perpetuate dualistic misconceptions and originate a vicious regress. Instead, as Garfield points out in his interpretation of Nāgārjuna's argument, to transcend the conventional samsaric (dualistic) perspective is to attain nirvāna and that attainment is "simply to see those things as they are – as merely empty, dependent, impermanent, and nonsubstantial."[153] It is in extinguishing all reifications, as obstacles to perceptual wholeness, that the original belief in separation is annihilated and one sees reality-as-it-is (i.e., enters nirvāna).

> Nāgārjuna surely thinks that in nirvāna, unlike samsāra, one perceives emptiness and not entities; one perceives the ultimate truth and not conventional truth. But emptiness of all entities, and the ultimate truth is merely the esssenceless essence of those conventional things. So nirvāna is only samsāra experienced as a Buddha experiences it. It is the person who enters nirvāna, but as a state of being, not as a place to be.[154]

It is clear in this last quote that nirvāna is not a physical (or otherwise) destination but, rather, a perspective that arises once the activity of reification comes to rest.

But how does that affect our interaction with a very real empirical world? Phenomena in the world, including our own subjectivity, do exist as empirical facts. In this sense, it is safe to say that both the individual and the Absolute, along with the possibility of a mystical union between the two, might very well exist also. Yet, all phenomena are conventional truths and saying this is simply another way "to characterize its mode of subsistence. It is to say that it is [as a conventional truth] without an independent nature."¹⁵⁵ *Empirical existence does not necessitate inherent existence.* While conventional existence might appear to contain instances of independent, inherent existence, these instances are ultimately empty. The mystical union between the individual and the Absolute represents to the individual an end to both the search for the Absolute as well as the end of him/herself as a separate identity in the conventional sense. This can be unsettling to any individual committed to maintaining a distinct notion of permanent or inherent existence in the world (i.e., an attachment to their own individual identity).

This also brings us back to the religious question raised at the beginning of this chapter by Nagao — more specifically, "who am I?" The point that needs to be recognized is that neither an inherent existence of the Absolute, nor that of the individual, can be asserted in the first place. There is no essential separation between the two and they exist as conceptions within conventional reality. When, from the conventional point of view, this becomes part of the individual's awareness and understanding then the conditioning effects of the phenomenal world are eroded.

> Having passed into nirvāna, the Victorious Conqueror
> Is neither said to be existent
> Nor said to be nonexistent.
> Neither both nor neither are said.
>
> So, when the victorious one abides, he
> Is neither said to be existent
> Nor said to be nonexistent.
> Neither both nor neither are said.
> (chapter XXV, verse 17-18)¹⁵⁶

Nonduality – A Mystical Union Between the Individual and the Absolute

Once the individual has entered into that state of awareness described as nirvāna, nothing more can be said about that individual's experience or existence. That is, the fact of their existence is only a temporal fact in the *conventional* sense. Likewise, the possibility of a mystical union between the individual and the Absolute can be spoken of only as a possibility within the perspective of *conventional* truth. To *actually* achieve this possibility requires the annihilation or extinction of one's own conception of the Absolute *and* of the individual's self-identity. One must be *empty* in relation to individual self-identity and this involves de-conditioning the individual consciousness from the process of reifying an independent 'self.' Once that reification of the separate psychological ego is ended, and reality is experienced *as it is* (i.e., nirvāna), it will be seen that the possibility for a mystical union between the individual and the Absolute never existed in the first place because the perceived separation between the two conventionally established entities was a mistaken view from the beginning.

In that sense, *the notions of the individual and the Absolute never existed as inherently existent and distinct beings in the ultimate sense and, therefore, can never ultimately unite.* The perceived separation that exists, according to Nāgārjuna's argument, is caused by the individual's conditioned belief in reified objects. Paradoxically, one could say that it is this belief in the notions of an inherently existent Absolute and an inherently existing self-identity that initially creates the experience (and tension) of separation. Where that belief ends, so too does the separation. This final point is expressed in one of Nāgārjuna's most paradoxical assertions:

> The pacification of all objectification
> And the pacification of illusion:

> No Dharma was taught by the Buddha
> At any time, in any place, to any person.
> (chapter XXV, verse 24)[157]

The ending of reification (i.e., the act of objectifying the world) ends the illusion presented in conventional truth. As a result, and from the point of view of *ultimate truth*, there can be no Buddha, no Dharma, and no Sangha. Certainly, these exist temporarily in the empirical sense but, as are all conventional truths, they are empty of inherent existence. With such a proclamation in hand, there is little left for the seeker than to follow through on Nāgārjuna's prescription for release from the conditions which, as was seen, originally gave rise to that urge to understand the nature of oneself and unite with the Absolute:

> The root of cyclic existence is action.
> Therefore, the wise does not act.
> Therefore, the unwise is the agent.
> The wise one is not because of his insight.
>
> With the cessation of ignorance
> Action will not arise.
> The cessation of ignorance occurs through
> Meditation and wisdom.
>
> Through the cessation of this and that
> This and that will not be manifest.
> The entire mass of suffering
> Indeed thereby completely ceases.
> (chapter XXVI, verse 10-12)[158]

This last statement could be considered one of the most important that Nāgārjuna could make in this context and can now be understood in light of what has been previously discussed. Nāgārjuna describes the conventional dualistic view of reality – that phenomena have distinct and inherent existence – as simply a mistaken view. He also demonstrates through his dialectic that all conceptualized 'things' are empty. The possibility for union between the individual and the Absolute is essentially a mistaken view and arises out of a naïve ignorance that leads to continuing actions in the dualistic sense. The cessation of ignorance and, hence, acting in the world as a distinct entity occurs through the cultivation of both meditation and wisdom (*prajñā*).

The term wisdom, or *prajñā*, denotes the development of a nondual perspective such that one can experience reality-as-it-is. Only by doing this is it possible to realize that ultimately everything, including one's own 'self,' has no inherent existence. This realization ends suffering and allows the individual to eventually perceive reality directly without subjective conditioning (i.e., to achieve nirvāna). By entering into the state of nirvāna, one then sees that the separation between the individual and the Absolute was only existent as an unrealizable desire within the confines of conventional truth.

It is clear from the analysis in this chapter that this final aspect of nondualism presented us with some problems in relations to Nāgārjuna's system of thought. Such a claim about union can only be made from what would be considered by Nāgārjuna to be the conventional view of reality. That is, such a possibility exists in the conventional sense where the notions of the individual and the Absolute exist temporarily. However, such reifications ultimately lack inherent existence and are therefore illusory and empty in the ultimate sense. The solution to this dilemma, according to the position laid out by Nāgārjuna, is to see that the perceived separation, which is at the root of our desire to unite with others, is an epistemological error and results in a mistaken view of reality. When one can end the process of reification and objectification then nondual reality-as-it-is arises.

This concludes the analysis of Nāgārjuna's *Mūlamadhyamakakārikā* utilizing the five aspects of nondualism described by David Loy. I have identified their presence throughout the work and from such an analysis it can be seen that Nāgārjuna's *Mūlamadhyamakakārikā* contains layers of thematic nondualism that are woven together to create the garment of emptiness espoused by Nāgārjuna. This provides us with a much greater understanding of the subtleties involved in Nāgārjuna's project as a whole and the analysis has shown that distinct stages of his dialectical process can be interpreted in the form of discrete nondualist categories in themselves.

The next chapter will bring attention to some of the striking parallels that exist between Nāgārjuna's philosophical position, as outlined previously, and other notions raised more recently within the field of quantum physics. Such a comparison will reveal not only the value of the preceding analysis of Nāgārjuna's text but that from that analysis some advances in the understanding of other fields of nondualist theory might ensue. For example, as each aspect of nondualism developed within Nāgārjuna's text, it became clear how the paradoxes, which tend to arise in most nondual metaphysical systems, could be preserved and maintained even while the contradictions within these categories become resolved.

Nonduality – A Mystical Union Between the Individual and the Absolute

As we discovered in Nāgārjuna's philosophical arguments, the distinctions between conventional and ultimate reality can be embraced in Nāgārjuna's arguments while, at the same time, the perceived contradiction between the two can be understood as mere illusions. With this in mind, it will be useful to examine some of the distinct parallels that exist between Nāgārjuna's philosophical position and quantum physics.

Nagarjuna, Nondualism and the Nature of Nothing

Parallels Between the *Mūlamadhyamakakārikā* and Quantum Physics

One of the key injunctions attributed to the Buddha throughout many of the Sutras is on "seeing things as they are." Of all the efforts that the neophyte might make, it was toward achieving this capability that all struggling disciples aspired. In one of countless repetitions on this point, the Buddha was adamant:

> And what is that which is the cause of liberation? Passionlessness is the answer.... And what is that which is the cause of passionlessness? Repulsion is the answer.... And what is that which is the cause of repulsion? The knowledge and the vision of things as they really are is the answer. Yea, I say that the knowledge-and-vision of things as they really are is causally associated with repulsion.[159]

It is mainly through the pursuit and attainment of "seeing things as they really are" that the disciple developed a peculiar form of repulsion or detachment to life's experiences and thereby achieved enlightenment or nirvāna. In an unexpected turn, it is this same goal to "see things as they are" that has now become the 21st century mantra heard throughout the field of research into quantum physics. In no other area in the sphere of contemporary scientific investigation could this statement be more accurately or appropriately expressed. In this sense, the goal of Mādhyamika philosophy has a critical relationship to the goals of quantum physics.

The analysis so far has provided a unique perspective on the nondualist arguments found within Nāgārjuna's work while, at the same time, expanding upon the subtle interwoven layers of nondualism within his philosophical system. The importance of such a nuanced understanding is critical to the development of other fields of nondualist research and speculation. From medicine (Dossey, 1989, 2000) and psychology (Mindell, 2000) (Wilbur, 1995) (Lawlis, 1996) (Mansfield, 1995), to the newest pronouncements in quantum theory (Herbert, 1987, 1993) (Friedman, 1990) (Wolf, 1981), it has become more apparent that a greater application and understanding of nonduality is required in order to move in any significant way beyond our present theoretical ground. That includes a greater understanding into just how the world interacts and functions as a whole at the quantum level.

An area of contemporary investigation that relies, in part, on the strengths of a nondualist metaphysic is the field of quantum physics; although many contradictions, which were resolved in Nāgārjuna's dialectic, continue to plague quantum theorists. This is due, in part, to the fact that contemporary science has focused its efforts on investigating the ontological status of the universe without first calling into question the epistemological limits of that investigation. Modern science continues to rely heavily upon empirical evidence while it is that empiricism itself that Nāgārjuna called into question from the beginning. This has made progress difficult for those within many fields of current research wherever those contradictions have arisen.

However, both the investigations of quantum physics and the outcome of Nāgārjuna's dialectic continue to find coherent explanations through a nondualist metaphysic despite the fact that they arrive at these conclusions through different approaches. It should not be surprising, then, that statements coming out from the community of theoretical physicists should exhibit a striking resemblance to the arguments and concepts expounded almost two thousand years earlier by Nāgārjuna. This is not to suggest, however, that the latter was in some way a derivative of the former, or even that the one was perhaps necessary in order for the other to come about. The similarities that these two compelling philosophical positions exhibit suggest that an important underlying relationship exists that might be mutually beneficial when evaluated in light of a nondualistic perspective.

The idea of identifying parallels between systems in Eastern philosophy and modern quantum physics is not new and in more recent years has even become part of the inspiration for the study of quantum physics, outside of that discipline. It gained widespread awareness in Western culture through such noted authors as Fritjof Capra. In the *Tao of Physics* he writes:

> The mystic looks within and explores his or her consciousness at its various levels, which include the body as the physical manifestation of the mind.... The mystic is aware of the wholeness of the entire cosmos.... In contrast to the mystic, the physicist begins his enquiry into the essential nature of things by studying the material world. Penetrating into ever deeper realms of matter, he has become aware of the essential unity of all things and events. More than that, he also learnt that he himself and his consciousness are an integral part of the unity. Thus the mystic and physicist arrive at the same conclusion; one starting from the inner realm, the other from the outer world.[160]

Shimon Malin, Professor of Physics at Colgate University, shares Capra's enthusiasm on the continued investigation of these parallels. "The philosophical implications of quantum mechanics have been the subject of a number of recent books that tend to emphasize connections between quantum physics and Eastern philosophy. I believe that investigations of such connections are important."[161]

For this reason, the bulk of this chapter will look at several of the essential characteristic features of nondualism that appear in both Nāgārjuna's nondualist philosophy and modern quantum theory. It is not within the realm of this chapter to elucidate the finer points of modern theoretical physics, nor is it my intention to provide a set of proofs that either confirm or deny the claims put forth by the respected scholars and mathematicians in each of the fields. Furthermore, it is admitted that some linguistic barriers exist between each of these disparate systems of thought and so one to one comparisons can be difficult at times. Nevertheless, I wish to draw attention to some of the striking parallels that exist between the *ideas* as they are expressed in these two distinct philosophical systems.

Ontological Nonduality

The first major parallel to be found is in the inevitability that the universe is fundamentally nondual. This simple correspondence should not be underestimated. Rather, it should be considered an exceptional event that there would be such a concurrence between these two unrelated fields. It has already been identified that Nāgārjuna's philosophical position implies the reality of a nondual ontology. While this is not *explicitly* stated in the *Mūlamadhyamakakārikā* his negation of the dualistic perspective is abundantly present and it has been thoroughly represented in previous chapters.

Quantum physics, on the other hand, is not as subtle in its assertions. As was stated previously, quantum physics has focused much of its research and investigative effort in directly examining the ontological reality of matter and, despite the obvious epistemological limits in this approach, has been able to demonstrate some of the nondual characteristics of the universe.

To provide an idea of how quantum physicists have had to reformulate their notions about the world we live in, David Albert, Professor of Philosophy at Columbia University, clarifies the essential position of modern theoretical physics:

> What needs to be changed is the fundamental ontology of the world. What you have to do is give up the idea that the material world consists of particles...and adopt the idea that it consists of something else...
> What goes on in relativistic quantum theories is that one imagines that there is an infinitely tiny physical system permanently located at every single mathematical point in the entirety of space; [that is] one imagines that there is literally an infinite array of such systems, one for each point. And each one of those infinitely tiny systems is stipulated to be a quantum-mechanical system. And each one of them is stipulated to interact in a particular way with each of its neighbors. And the complete array of them is called the field.[162]

This is a strange concept for one with a dualistic perspective to accommodate. Part of the difficulty is due to the fact that it is problematical for the mind to juggle with the 'size' or 'quantity' of *infinity*, dealing as it does with finite object-oriented thinking. Infinity, in the material world, means *everything*. That is, an infinite amount of any 'thing' means that it must eventually exist everywhere and in all things. Any notion of infinity immediately rebels against the dualist view that there could be something *else* which can be distinguished from that infinite thing. That is, if there could be a single object apart from the infinite thing, then that infinite thing couldn't really be called infinite. But if there *is* an infinite thing then the dualist explanation of reality doesn't work as a model for existence either.

David Bohm was one of the foremost thinkers and theoretical physicists of his generation. Chief amongst his views on the connection between consciousness and matter was the notion that each instance, moment, or region of space "contains a total structure 'enfolded' within it."[163] Much like the characteristics described by Albert, every region of space contains a sense of order similar to that which is enfolded in all other regions of space. Furthermore, this implies that some form of underlying order or wholeness pervades and influences the operation of the universe on a macrocosmic scale. He calls this the enfolded or *implicate* order. To illustrate this Bohm recalls an example of a fascinating laboratory experiment:

> A more striking example of implicate order can be demonstrated in the laboratory, with a transparent container full of a very viscous fluid, such as treacle, and equipped with a mechanical rotator that can 'stir' the fluid very slowly but very thoroughly. If an insoluble droplet of ink is placed in the fluid and the stirring device is set in motion, the ink drop is gradually transformed

into a thread that extends over the whole fluid. The latter now appears to be distributed more or less at 'random' so that it is seen as some shade of grey. But if the mechanical stirring device is now turned in the opposite direction, the transformation is reversed, and the droplet of dye suddenly appears, reconstituted.

When the dye was distributed in what appeared to be a random way, it nevertheless had *some kind* of order which is different, for example, from that arising from another droplet originally placed in a different position. But this order is *enfolded* or *implicated* in the 'grey mass' that is visible in the fluid. Indeed, one could thus 'enfold' a whole picture."[164]

The immediate thought that comes to mind is of the myriad of stars and galaxies scattered throughout the universe, like droplets of ink, spreading out from the original 'picture' to form one universal matrix. Bohm's notion of an implicate order suggests that if at some point the cosmic 'stirring apparatus' reverses, the universe could revert to some original pattern or state which revealed the implicate order of all things. The example he provided previously illustrates the idea of just such an order. More importantly, it suggests an unbroken connection between all things in the universe. As Bohm asserts, "the primary emphasis is now on *undivided wholeness*, in which the observing instrument is not separate from what is observed."[165]

Werner Heisenberg was abundantly clear on the notion of the essential unity of all matter:

> All the elementary particles can, at sufficiently high energies, be transmuted into other particles, or they can be simply created from kinetic energy

and can be annihilated into energy, for instance into radiation. Therefore, we have here actually the final proof for the unity of matter. All the elementary particles are made of the same substance, which we may call energy or universal matter; they are just different forms in which matter can appear.[166]

That all things in the universe are energy is the simplest expression of nonduality that one can have and it has been the basis of scientific understanding for almost a century now. It is the central assertion that allowed Albert Einstein to develop the special theory of relativity, and through which Werner Heisenberg was able to cultivate quantum mechanics.

Henry Stapp, Professor of Physics at the Lawrence Berkeley Laboratory, University of California, also weighs in with his arguments on the necessity of viewing reality nondually: "The conceptual framework of quantum theory...allows minds and matter to be seen as the natural part of a single whole."[167] This is an important feature that classical physics seems incapable of adopting. In fact, as Stapp explains, "classical physics has, as is well known, no rational place for consciousness: it is already logically complete."[168] That is to say, there is no place in classical physics to rationally account for consciousness and it must be 'inserted' into classical theory 'by hand.' "The logical situation in quantum theory is quite different: there is an absolute logical need for something else, such as consciousness."[169]

The necessity to integrate and unify consciousness into the quantum equation is reiterated by Euan Squires. Essentially, according to quantum theory, it is the *way* that we observe the world that determines *what* we end up observing.[170] Amit Goswami goes further to indicate that "the philosophy of monistic idealism provides a paradox-free interpretation of quantum physics that is logical, coherent, and satisfying."[171] In this sense it seems realistically plausible to develop a coherent scientific view of the world, which includes the paradoxical nature of the quantum world, only if we adopt a monistic or nondual perspective. Not only is metaphysics obligated to work within this nondual position, it is encouraged to admit "a level of reality at which the experiencer is inseparable from what's experienced as reality."[172] The fact that science is moved to accept that the essential characteristic of reality is nondual provides a strikingly parallel conclusion to that defended in Nāgārjuna's dialectical treatise. This nondualist outlook brings forth a second major point – the notion that individuals can no longer persist in distinguishing themselves as autonomous independent beings, distinct from the rest of reality.

Subject-Object Interdependence

The conscious subjective experience of the world is generally accepted to be one of the primary representations of truth that idealizes an individual's autonomy as a distinct 'being'. Based on this substantially *empirical* perspective, laws governing the protection of the private citizen, including personal rights for one's own individuality, have been drafted throughout the centuries to affirm what is considered this most basic of all observable facts – the autonomy of the human individual. Our immediate experience of reality is exemplified in Descartes' characterization of the individual as *res cogitans* or 'a thinking thing.' According to Nāgārjuna, however, our presumed status as an autonomous subjective thinker is actually empty of any *inherent* individual existence. *The "I" possesses no substantial permanent existence but simply arises dependently and reflexively in the mind's eye upon other conditions that are themselves empty.* Likewise, the instances of 'subject' and 'object' are only conditions that exist interdependently:

> Someone is disclosed by something.
> Something is disclosed by someone.
> Without something how can someone exist?
> Without someone how can something exist?
> (chapter IX, verse, 5)[173]

The observer and the observed cannot be said to have inherent existence such that they could exist independently of one another. Quantum physics makes much the same claim and links the dependency of the observer and observed just as explicitly as Nāgārjuna does:

> In the most widely accepted view of quantum theory, called the Copenhagen interpretation, it's held that what we experience as physical reality doesn't exist in a definite or determinate state before observation and that it's the act of observation itself which somehow defines or determines the state of physical reality.[174]

This is an important statement that shows a striking resemblance to Nāgārjuna's earlier claim. Quantum physics asserts that the state of the observed object is determined by, and through, the observer. In other words, they arise dependently. This idea is substantiated further in the Heisenberg Uncertainty Principle. Paul Davies describes this principle and what it means to us:

> It [the Heisenberg Uncertainty Principle] says you can't know where an atom, or electron, or whatever, is located *and* know how it is moving, at one and the same time. Not only can you not know it, but the very concept of an atom with a definite location and motion is meaningless."[175]

This is reminiscent of Nāgārjuna's assertions about the mistaken notion that an object exists inherently or that it has motion. As early as chapter II in the *Mūlamadhyamakakārikā*, Nāgārjuna steers his logical dialectic to the following conclusion:

> Neither an entity nor a nonentity
> Moves in any of the three ways.
> So motion, mover,
> And route are nonexistent.
> (chapter II, verse 25)[176]

The Heisenberg Uncertainty Principle would defend a similar conclusion. That is, there is no actual moment where one can pinpoint both the actual physical existence of an object *and* describe its movement. Such uncertainty puts both existence and motion into question.

> According to Bohr, the fuzzy and nebulous world of the atom only sharpens into concrete reality when an observation is made. In the absence of an observation, the atom is a ghost. It only materializes when you look for it. And you decide what to look for. Look for its location and you get an atom in place. Look for its motion and you get an atom with a speed. But you can't have both.[177]

Davies is stressing here that at no time will you be able to identify an atom and its movement as a complete event. That is, you may be able to mathematically determine an instance of 'atom' and you may, at another time, be able to determine an instance of 'motion,' but you can never determine the instance of a 'moving-atom' (i.e. position *and* motion). It simply doesn't exist despite our persistent desire for an epistemological interpretation of reality in those terms. As Nāgārjuna would simply assert, our view of reality is mistaken and consists merely of conventional truth without inherent existence.

This brings us back to the notion of the Absolute or Universal Mind in Buddhist ontology. Nirvāṇa, as Nāgārjuna has implied, is simply reality-as-it-is without the interference of a particular subjective perspective or interpretation imposed upon it by the reified subject (i.e., observer). From this standpoint, there can be no absolute distinction made between the observer and the observed, or subject and object. Consciousness, which is believed to be inherently existent and autonomous whilst subjectified within the human being is, upon achieving nirvāṇa, experienced as a part of a much larger whole (if one can be forgiven in employing such a dualistic description of a nondualist experience).

While disagreement exists to some extent within the field of quantum physics, many mainstream theorists have likewise begun to accept certain fundamental notions about the nature of consciousness. These notions include the view that the very nature of the universe itself is conscious.

> If one respects the truths of science and believes that they do provide us with an improved

understanding of the conditions for our being and becoming in the vast cosmos, then narrowly anthropomorphic conceptions of the character of Being, or of reality-in-itself, do not seem commensurate with the 'vision' of physical reality contained in modern physical theory. What this vision does allow us, in our view, to safely 'infer,' without, very importantly, being able to 'prove,' is that the universe is conscious. If one can accept this argument, then the profound sense of alienation that has seemingly been occasioned by the success of classical physics from the eighteenth century to the present could be rather dramatically alleviated.[178]

Not only are we getting a picture in quantum physics that the subject and object are vitally interdependent, but it can be seen that the subjective consciousness actually shares, in an intimate way, in the essential consciousness that *is* the universe.

Charles Bennett, a Fellow at the IBM Thomas J. Watson Research Center, disagrees with the notions held by Kafatos, Nadeau, Goswami, and others, that the ground of being for the universe is consciousness. Bennett, who spearheaded and developed quantum teleportation research (and produced the first successes in teleportation) suggests that quantum physics can be explained without resorting to metaphysics. Nevertheless, such 'metaphysical' theories remain prominent among theorists today and exhibit parsimony and rigour, not to mention a certain degree of charm that is hard to ignore. As Kafatos and Nadeau suggested earlier, the sense of alienation, which occurs within individuals, is occasioned by the *belief* that they are somehow separate from the totality of consciousness in the universe. The implications now, as a result of rigorous experimentation, are that we are an integral part of an underlying universal matrix.[179] This reiterates the view held by Nāgārjuna that there is no distinction between the subject and object, or between an individual's consciousness and the One Mind, other than what arises as our conventional view of reality. The notion of the interdependence of both subject and object is, therefore, substantially present in both philosophical positions.

The Two-Aspect Model of Reality

This particular notion embraces the view that there exists, at the very least, two distinct interpretations or experiences of reality. It is important from the outset to distinguish the fact that this does not mean that there actually *are* two simultaneous empirical universes existing side-by-side. Rather, that while there is only one reality, there seem to be at least two distinct ways that this singular reality can be experienced. Essentially, this is an epistemological rather than ontological problem for the perceiver. According to Nāgārjuna, these two experientially distinctive perspectives of reality consist of either the experience of reality-as-it-is, unconditioned by the subjective mind, or of reality as it would be experienced whilst under the influences and conditioning of a subjective interpretation of reality. This 'two-aspects' model of reality, as I prefer to call it, goes variously under the names ultimate/conventional truth, nirvāna/samsāra, unconditioned/conditioned reality, reality-as-it-is/subjective reality, Absolute/relative, and many others. Modern physics has its own version of this distinction and is characterized primarily by the terms classical/quantum world, or particle/wave physics. While these paired names represent distinctively different notions about the universe, they all represent an approach to reality which acknowledges that there is one way in which the world actually exists and another artificial or illusory way in which we epistemologically experience it.

This is an important notion and one that should not be dismissed without serious investigation. Nāgārjuna described our dualistic experience of reality as 'conventional' truth. Further, he identified the notion of 'ultimate' reality as the result of direct unconditioned experience. In the same vein, quantum physics accepts the reality of both a world that is observed by an observer who imposes a conditioned result on that experience (i.e., conventional truth), and an existence of that same reality when it is not conditioned by subjective observation. This second (ultimate) truth, a universe whose nature is consciousness itself, is the interconnected whole implied in Nāgārjuna's dialectic.

> Modern physics is moving toward understanding the universe as an interconnected whole. Concepts associated with quantum theory, such as nonlocality, point toward an underlying level of reality wherein what we experience as the separate material objects of physical reality are really inseparable and so must be connected or interconnected. In addition, the concept of wave/particle duality associated with quantum theory points toward a level of reality which the experiencer is inseparable from what's experienced as reality.[180]

Arnold Mindell, a graduate of MIT and the Jung Institute in Zurich, suggests that our essential psychological interconnectedness is presently being rediscovered and that current experiments are beginning to unlock the fascinating potential of the human mind. "Until now this interconnectedness has defied the sense of linear time and locality and has been called by many names, such as déjà vu, synchronicity, and God."[181] It is more than curious, for instance, to consider how little attention has been paid, comparatively speaking, to Jung's investigations into the notion of *synchronicity*.[182]

More than any one thing, however, interconnectedness may have profound implications for the way we may come to deal with the world and our relationships with others.

> All we can say at present is that locality or spatial separation of the particles is no longer a meaningful concept. Particles no longer have a separate locality. There is no simple analogy for this 'non-locality' of entangled quantum objects in everyday life, except that none of us lives in a separate reality.... At the level of our deepest, most sentient, subtle experiences, we are entangled.[183]

Mindell's use of the term 'entangled' is meant to suggest that there is no separation between objects in the ultimate sense, and any action in one distinct area of space must, by definition, have effects on all areas of space. Nāgārjuna's philosophical system would certainly be able to accommodate a statement such as 'entangled' within the scope of conventional truth. From the quantum mechanical side of the argument, we are presented with the notion of *nonlocality* to describe the fundamental state of reality with its substantive interconnectedness. Nonlocality represents one of the most profound paradigm-destroying conceptions facing classical physicists today. Kaufman provides a simple view of this principle:

> Quantum theory predicts a phenomenon called nonlocality, whereby observation and determination of the state of one particle simultaneously affects the state of another, distant particle, no matter how far apart those particles are. Thus, even though there's an apparent spatial separation between the particles, quantum theory predicts a more subtle level of interconnection, a nonspatial, or nonlocal, connection. This theoretical effect was experimentally demonstrated in what are called the Aspect experiments, after the French quantum physicist Alain Aspect.[184]

The idea of nonlocality describes the characteristic of the instantaneous signal-less transmission of information between objects, regardless of the distance between those two objects. It is essentially the ability to send signals between any two points in the universe instantaneously (i.e., faster than the speed of light). The difficulty for us is that within the current model of classical physics, as well as from our dualistic perspective of reality, this instantaneous signal-less transmission should not be possible between two distinct objects. Einstein referred to this phenomenon as "spooky action at a distance."[185] and Kaufman suggests that our ability to understand it can arise if we come to appreciate the fact that no separation existed between those objects in the first place. This pronouncement echoes the notions implied in Nāgārjuna's dialectic. Kaufman explains his own thinking on the idea of interconnectedness:

> While this separation may appear to be real at one level of reality, at the experiential level of reality,

> if space-time is a relational matrix,...then that separation isn't actually or ultimately real because it doesn't operate at the fundamental level of reality from which physical reality extends.[186]

Kaufman is really describing two levels of *experience* here within one ontological system. There is the level of reality that we experience (conventional truth) which is dualistically framed and can be described through the model of classical physics. But that dualistic perspective on reality, as Kaufman further suggests, does not "operate at the more fundamental level of reality."[187] At the *actual* level of reality (ultimate truth) "nonlocality exists because what we observe as separate particles aren't ultimately separable entities, and so they can function in some ways as a single unit."[188] We can then begin to understand the essential characteristics of our universe if we formulate the assumption about particles in space that "they're not actually separate, but only appear to be separate because we can't perceive the relational spatial structure from which they extend and through which they're connected, and which thereby unifies them."[189]

Finally, by bringing our minds to adopt such a perspective on reality we will be able to posit that the characteristic of space-time "functions as a relational matrix and that one of the properties of a relational matrix is this underlying unity and interconnection between its relational parts."[190]

This is a common conclusion within the field of quantum physics although, admittedly, it is not yet universally accepted amongst peers. However, the notions expressed here remain the opinion of many within the community of quantum theorists and provide a striking similarity to Nāgārjuna's position on time and space.

In the *Mūlamadhyamakakārikā*, Nāgārjuna examines both time (Chapter XIX) and the subsequent notion of distance or space (Chapters VIII, XI, XIV) and, with his use of the Tetralemma, finds them all empty of inherent existence. That is, the ideas of time and space arise dependently as a result of an epistemological process (i.e., *pratītya-samputpāda*, or 'the twelve links') which substantiates our simple perception of ourselves as inherently existing. It is clear, then, that there is a congruence in the expression of two aspects or experiential levels of reality – Conventional/particle truth and Ultimate/wave truth – and that this 'two-aspect' interpretation of reality has been used as a tool that has aided both Nāgārjuna's dialectic and quantum theory to interpret the nature of the universe and our limited experience of it. On this one point have the two distinct philosophical positions, separated by nearly two millennia, benefited greatly toward establishing their respective, and somewhat compatible, positions.

The Tetralemma

No comparison of this sort would be complete without a look at the logical systems at work in both Nāgārjuna's dialectic and the logical methods confronting quantum theorists. I am speaking specifically of the *Tetralemma*, or *catuskoṭi*. This four-branched logical approach is central to Nāgārjuna's dialectic and, as we will see, has come to play an important central role in understanding the issues facing quantum physicists.

The early Greek philosophers often favoured the use of the *dilemma*, or two-branched logic of 'either/or,' which allowed them to negate seemingly paradoxical conclusions.[191] Dualistic in its approach, this common form of Aristotelian logic provided a method of enquiry that found its greatest expression and achievement in the form of classical (Newtonian) physics. This led to a further institutionalization of the dualist perspective (sometimes called the materialist or empiricist perspective), which subsequently produced enormous technological and cultural advances. However, there were certain limitations to this method that were not widely accepted at the time as limitations or shortfalls. Alfred North Whitehead expands on the difficulties faced by empirical scientific methods or by what he calls the *method of difference* (i.e. 'either/or'):

> Philosophers can never hope to finally formulate metaphysical first principles. Weakness of insight and deficiencies of language stand in the way inexorably...[although] there is no first principle which is in itself unknowable, not to be captured by a flash of insight...
>
> [However] the difficulty has its seat in the empirical side of philosophy. Our datum is the actual world, including ourselves; and this actual world spreads itself for observation in the guise of the topic of our immediate experience. The elucidation of immediate experience is the sole justification for any thought; and the starting-point for thought is the analytic observation of components of this experience.... We habitually observe by the method of difference. Sometimes we see an elephant, and sometimes we do not. The result is that an elephant, when present, is noted. Facility of observation depends on the fact that the object observed is important when present, and sometimes is absent.[192]

This is a damning statement by Whitehead against the over-reliance on empiricism and sensory interpretation in relation to metaphysical determinations, and this point accounts for some of the difficulties that continue to plague some quantum physicists. The 'method of difference', as Whitehead refers to it, keeps the investigation confined mainly within the limits of the human sensory apparatus and investigations about the world and reality almost always begin with the observation of the world and any changes that occur within that observed state. This can only serve to ensure that any conclusion that might eventually be derived from such an investigation will be naturally and necessarily dualistic. While it is a valid approach when attempting to develop a gross understanding of the empirical world, it should not be immediately assumed that it could yield *ultimate* metaphysical or ontological answers about the nature of reality. The only thing that we can be sure about with this method is that it can substantiate the limits of what falls into the spectrum of human observation, which is really to say nothing at all. By deconstructing the epistemological question Nāgārjuna was able to avoid some of these contradictions.

John Barrow, author of *Theories of Everything* and *The Artful Universe*, suggests that "universes that are complex enough to give rise to consciousness impose limits on what can be known about them from within."[193] This may be true as long as one stays attached to the conventional view of reality, and an opportunity to transcend our present dualistic point of view would certainly provide the litmus test for such a statement. But this does not make ultimate reality any more effable from a conventional perspective.

The limitation that we face from within the dualistic framework is partly responsible for making quantum physics such a contentious topic in the first place, and why some of its characteristics simply defy common dualistic descriptions and explanations. The fundamental conclusion of quantum physics is that research into the metaphysical nature of reality can no longer rest on the assumption that 'appearance equals reality.' Because of this one essential condition, we need to adopt new strategies of approach in such topics. This means that there is a need to develop, reinforce, and utilize systems of logic which will take us beyond the traditional black-and-white categories of 'either/or.' Quantum physics has had to do just that and has utilized a method of logic in its research that was once (and still is) the central component of Mādhyamika philosophy – namely, the Tetralemma.

This part of our journey requires a clearer understanding of the structure of the Tetralemma. The fourfold argument presents us with a series of propositions from which to question the inherent existence of any entity. The possible ways to view an entity that is claimed to be inherently existent are that it 'exists,' 'it does not exist,' 'it both exists and does not exist,' and 'it neither exists nor does not exist.' These exhaust the possibilities of its potential status in the world. The logical argument in symbolic form is as follows:

(1) X = Is
(2) $-X$ = Is Not
(3) $X * -(X)$ = both Is and Is Not
(4) $-X * -(-X)$ = neither Is nor Is Not

Florin Giripescu Sutton further explains this formula, familiar to us by now from earlier discussions:

> Note how thoroughgoing this type of logic is: it not only includes the two basic opposite alternatives of the classical either/or dilemma, but it also operates with a combination of the two, either conjunctively or disjunctively (both affirmation and negation, or neither affirmation nor negation). In addition, one has also the option of denying all four alternatives, in which case another, transcendental dimension will be created, which stands in opposition to all four, taken either individually or together.[194]

This 'meaty' challenge against the inherent existence of objects includes not only the essential empiricist perspective of 'either/or,' or 'is/is not,' but includes additional categories of consideration which exemplify more subtle modes of existence.[195] In relation to Nāgārjuna's use of the Tetralemma, Nagao has the following to say:

> Catuskoti consists of any four alternative propositions such as, for example, 'exist,' 'does not exist,' 'both exists and does not exist,' and 'neither exists nor does not exist.' It is observed that the existence of all things is summed up and represented by these four propositions and that, dialectically speaking, there is no other possibility. Nāgārjuna's argument consists of probing into whether each proposition can stand on its own. Through this examination, he attempts to point out that if a proposition is stated with a belief in a 'self-nature,' that is, if it is based on a substantive realistic view, it necessarily falls into a contradiction of antinomy [i.e. a contradiction between two equally binding laws or logical conclusions] and cannot stand on its own. Therefore he concludes that if a proposition is to

be established, it must have 'no self-nature,' that is, it must be empty."[196]

This general principle of logic eventually led to a reference to Nāgārjuna and his followers as teachers of the 'Middle Path' (Mādhyamika) – between 'being' and 'non-being.' As Sutton points out, this is exactly the logical position needed for Nāgārjuna to 'imply' an alternative to the reality that we experience. It is also what allows him to continually erode our epistemological interpretation of reality. "This fourfold negation is a metaphysical category, which the Buddhists are very fond of using in discussing ultimate matters, and which they call Voidness (Śūnyatā)."[197]

The important aspect of the previous passage is that researchers in the field of quantum physics also employ this same formula to describe their understanding of quantum reality. Albert describes the results of a typical quantum experiment that was designed to describe a specific characteristic of an atom (in this example, 'hardness' or 'softness') *while* it is moving through an apparatus that measures its motion. As we will recall from an earlier discussion on the Heisenberg Uncertainty Principle that we cannot know the position of a particle *and* the motion or momentum of that particle at the same time. The result of measuring the motion of the atom, paradoxically, puts our certainty about the existent characteristics of that same atom in question. Also, as suggested by Sutton previously, negating the four categories of possible existence opens up the possibility of a new transcendental category. Albert describes for us the view on this from the perspective of quantum physics:

Parallels Between the *Mūlamadhyamakakārikā* and Quantum Physics

> Electrons seem to have modes of being, or modes of moving, available to them which are quite unlike what we know how to think about…. The name of that new mode (which is just a name for something we don't understand) is *superposition*. What we say about an…electron which is now passing through our apparatus…is that it's not on *h* [hard] and not on *s* [soft] and not on both and not on neither, but, rather, that it's in a superposition of being on *h and* being on *s*. And what that means (other than 'none of the above') we don't know.[198]

It is clear in this exposition that Albert is essentially describing the quantum view of matter in terms that utilize the Tetralemma. The electron is neither hard, nor soft, nor both, nor neither, but is described as existing in *superposition*. *Superposition* appears to be that new transcendent sphere, suggested by Sutton, which arises once the four arms of the Tetralemma have been negated. This explanation offers the same antinomy described earlier by Nagao.

By correspondence, and according to the conclusions suggested in Nāgārjuna's dialectic, the model of superposition given in the explanation above would indicate that *the electron is essentially 'empty' of any inherent existence of its own but arises dependently, and temporarily, upon conditions within the environment.* This congruent view has important implications for the individual as it also implies the temporality and emptiness of the material 'self.'[199] It is through the use of the Tetralemma in both philosophical systems that the notion of the emptiness of phenomena is similarly expressed.

I have attempted to show the striking parallels that exist between the notions raised by Nāgārjuna in his philosophy of emptiness and the conclusions exemplified in the same logical processes of quantum physics. These parallels suggest that much more can be shared between the essential philosophical views of Eastern philosophy and those of modern physics. I have not meant to suggest in any way that the conclusions derived through quantum physics were somehow established first by Nāgārjuna almost two thousand years ago, for each system retains its own unique subtleties. However, the scientific community might benefit greatly through an understanding of the subtleties expressed in Nāgārjuna's metaphysical system. That these two vastly different fields can evidence such congruence speaks to the possibility, perhaps, that some of the greatest thinkers in history, both past and present, have identified essential features of reality that commonly elude our day to day experience.

Conclusion

Having utilized the five aspects of nondualism articulated by David Loy, I have clearly identified their presence within Nāgārjuna's *Mūlamadhyamakakārikā*. I am not claiming that Nāgārjuna intended to develop his nondualist arguments based upon the five-category schema. However, it was through the use of this template that I was able to more easily identify the subtly interwoven aspects of nondualist thought embedded throughout his work. Additionally, it brings a new perspective to Nāgārjuna's arguments in a way that makes the complexity of his dialectical process more obvious. That this categorical analysis works so well is a tribute to the intricate and thorough nature of Nāgārjuna's original work.

The first aspect, *the negation of dualist thinking*, is essential to the foundation of any nondualist philosophical position and, for that reason, we see Nāgārjuna supporting this position from the outset. His dialectic utilizes the Tetralemma as a way of demonstrating the illogic of dualist thinking, despite the fact that the dualist position constitutes the line of least resistance for an empirical experience of the world. The tendency to describe the world according to how it is *appears to the senses* leads to explanations about the world that will tend only to validate those particular sensory perspectives. That is, we often exhibit a tendency to make our metaphysical interpretations of reality fit our epistemological experience and empirical observations. From this empirical perspective comes the tendency to assign inherent and essential existence to ourselves, as subjects, and to other 'things' in the world, as objects. As Nāgārjuna has pointed out, this is an illusory and mistaken (although understandable) interpretation of reality. We experience the world dualistically but our best logical arguments indicate that the world cannot be inhabited by any independent or inherent existences. The arguments by Nāgārjuna suggest that all things arise dependently and exist only conventionally.

The second aspect, *the nonplurality of the world*, flows naturally from the first aspect. If it can be shown that the notion of relations between objects is logically incoherent then we must also call into question the idea of plurality. As Whitehead maintains, we often limit our explanations and explorations of the world by what we are able to describe through observation. However, it requires a great deal of mental effort to maintain a view that is contrary to our unremitting sensory experience of the world. Needless to say, this effort is necessary if we are to come to understand that the notion of 'relations' between apparently distinct objects is logically impossible, and that the distinction is merely observational. This view by Nāgārjuna is further corroborated in the logical arguments made by F. H. Bradley. Nāgārjuna brings the notion of a nonplural world into focus and has provided a substantial argument through which to ground his assertion.

The third aspect, *the nondifference of subject and object*, is a logical deduction that arises out from the previous points. More than that, however, Nāgārjuna establishes the incoherence of believing in either the subject or the object as entities that are independent and autonomous within any framework of reality. This two-fold attack against anything that an individual mind might attempt to establish as 'real' is designed to illustrate that the things which can be *conceived* of by the mind as real are, in fact, empty. Furthermore, he makes the point that it is inadequate to simply collapse either the subject into the object or vice versa. While those approaches have been used variously in unrelated nondualist positions throughout history, it is clear by Nāgārjuna's argument that neither the object nor the subject can be claimed to be existent if one is hoping to ultimately establish a true and coherent view of reality. That is, neither subject nor object can be said to exist in the ultimate sense and each are empty and arise dependently upon the other.

This last line of reasoning brought us to an understanding of the fourth aspect of nondualism – *the identity of phenomenon and the Absolute*. If the previous stance can be maintained – that there is no difference between subject and object – then it follows, as a consequence, that there is no true distinction between phenomenon and the Absolute. That is, a difference exists empirically in the conventional sense, but there can be no distinction made ultimately. This is often referred to as 'the nonduality of duality and nonduality' and Nāgārjuna's position is epitomized by the claim that 'samsāra is nirvāna.' There is *one* world, and our experience of that one reality will vary according to the conditioned mind through which it is experienced. Release from samsāra is a matter of de-conditioning one's mind from that reifying dualistic perspective in order to directly experience reality-as-it-is.

This brings us to our fifth and final aspect of nondualism. Given the principles utilized by Nāgārjuna in the first four categories, there then exists, as seen from the *conventional* point of view, the possibility of a *mystical union between the individual, or phenomena, and the Absolute*. This statement, however, must be seen in context of the fact that what we call the individual and what we call the Absolute were never *ultimately* existent or separate from each other. Nāgārjuna's dialectical position implies that the achievement of unity in this aspect of nondualism is not a consequence of bringing together, in the positive sense, of two actual entities (i.e., such as the individual with the Absolute), but arises out of the negation of the original belief that there even existed such a separation between the individual and the Absolute. It should be further understood that this does not deny an ultimate ground of being, nor does it deny the need for religion as a tool for growth and relationship within *conventional* reality. Rather, this viewpoint maintains that the conviction in a perceived split between the individual and the Absolute is a fundamental conceptual error, and that an essential underlying unity does exist despite its apparent eclipse by our sensory and/or cerebral apparatus.

Perhaps this is the original sin of humanity – its self-imposed exile from 'paradise'. Having 'eaten' from the 'tree of knowledge' (i.e., achieved consciousness self-awareness and identity-gathering capability), humanity began a period of mental activity wherein we began to habitually identify ourselves as separate subjective entities. We then became experientially blind and lost sight of ultimate truth (i.e. our interconnected place in 'Eden'). The human project starts with a fall from Grace (or nirvāna) which sets the stage for a long and painful struggle back to that original state of enlightenment or realization. The human experience, then, becomes underwritten from the beginning by that sense of separation from the Absolute, or God. At this point, such a view must remain conjecture, although it presents a compelling idea.

Conclusion

As I indicated earlier, the nondualist perspective would describe the individual and the Absolute similarly; as mere expressions of one underlying universal consciousness. However, it would contradict Nāgārjuna's dialectical position to make the claim that an individual identity was in any way synonymous with the Absolute, for that would likewise be asserting the continued existence of an essential 'I'. The alternative is to recognize that concepts of both the individual and the Absolute are simply illusions derived from an epistemological error in the perception of reality, and that they are not independently existent but are empty of inherent existence and arise dependently as empirical, although temporary, phenomena.

The five aspects of nondualism have given us a much deeper insight into the subtlety of Nāgārjuna's work. As I explained at the beginning, it is difficult to provide a single definition of nonduality that will render a true sense and full understanding of nondualism. The analysis of Nāgārjuna's *Mūlamadhyamakakārikā* provides a vehicle through which to articulate the nuances contained within the complex of nondual conceptions.

Following that analysis, I presented a series of four striking parallels between the philosophical position held in Nāgārjuna's philosophical treatise and that held in contemporary quantum physics. From this, the congruence of ideas can be seen in four main areas including: the two-aspect model of reality, ontological nonduality, ontological interdependence, and a similarity in the methods of argument and explanation utilizing the Tetralemma.

Despite the disparity existing between these two unrelated fields of thought, these basic agreements can still be found to exist between the two. The similarity ensures that a case can be made for further comparison and cooperation between these distinct, and yet dynamic, philosophical positions.

It is my hope and expectation that humanity continues to advance in its growing awareness of the integral whole, and that a moment of clarity will one day shatter the chains of dualism that bind and enslave our present experience of reality. That this dualistic experience has caused humanity much suffering is an understatement of great import. That we are capable of overcoming this illusion by developing a new way of living and experiencing reality is critical to the continued existence of the human race on this planet. I hope that this work can make some contribution to that evolution.

Endnotes

Introduction

1. Geoffrey Samuel, <u>Civilized Shamans: Buddhism in Tibetan Societies</u>. (Washington: Smithsonian Institution Press, 1993) 396.
2. Edward Conze, <u>Buddhism: Its Essence and Development</u>. (New York: Harper & Row, Publishers, 1959) 134.
3. G. M. Nagao, <u>Mādhyamika and Yogācāra: A Study of Mahāyāna Philosophies</u>. (Delhi: Sri Satguru Publications, 1991) xi.
4. Nagao, xi.
5. Garfield's translation is from the Tibetan version (of the original Sanskrit) called the *dBu-ma rsta-ba shes-rab*. Garfield recounts that this is the text read by and commented upon by generations of Tibetan philosophers.
6. Every cited instance from Garfield's translation of the *Mūlamadhyamakakārikā* includes both a page reference for his book as well as the chapter and verse reference.
7. Jay L. Garfield is a "Professor of Philosophy and Director of the Hampshire in India Program (an exchange program with the Tibetan universities in exile) at Hampshire College."
8. Christian Lindtner, <u>Journal of the American Oriental Society</u>, vol. 108, 1988: 178.
9. David Loy, <u>Nonduality: A Study in Comparative Philosophy</u>. (New York: Humanity Books, 1988) 189.
10. Samuel, 39.
11. Jaidev Singh, <u>An Introduction to Madhyamaka Philosophy</u>. (Delhi: Motilal Banarsidass, 1968) 21-22.
12. David Seyfort Ruegg, <u>A History of Indian Literature: The Literature of the Madhyamaka School of Philosophy in India</u>. (Wiesbaden: Harrasowitz, 1981) 48-49.
13. Ruegg, <u>A History of Indian Literature</u>, 49.

Problems in Defining Nondualism

14. Jay Garfield, <u>The Fundamental Wisdom of the Middle Way: Nāgārjuna's *Mūlamadhyamakakārikā*.</u> (New York: Oxford University Press, 1995) 330-31.
15. Christian Lindtner, <u>Nagarjuniana: Studies in the Writings and Philosophy of Nāgārjuna</u>. (Delhi: Motilal Banarsidass, 1982) 269.
16. This point has often resulted in a premature or unnecessary criticism of eastern philosophy by western scholars. The goal or intent of many eastern writings is toward liberation or release. This can shift the emphasis within the writings in ways that lead to misunderstandings by interpreters who lack an appreciation for this goal.
17. Paul Hacker, <u>Philology and Confrontation</u>. Edited by Wilhelm Halbfass. (New York: State University of New York Press, 1995) 138.
18. Garfield, 270.
19. The notion of 'scientific objectivity' has come into question within the field of quantum physics and the Heisenberg Uncertainty Principle would suggest that you cannot separate the observer and the observed. Objectivity, while it is important in dealing with conventional truth, seems to be nothing more than opinion when considering ultimate truth. This will be discussed more in detail later.
20. Erich Frauwallner, <u>History of Indian Philosophy</u>. (Delhi: Motilal Banarsidass, 1973) 95.
21. Frauwallner, 34.
22. <u>Wisdom of the Buddha: The Unabridged Dhammapada</u>. Edited and translated by F. Max Müller. (New York: Dover Publications, Inc., 2000) 81.
23. E. Obermiller, "The Sublime Science of the Great Vehicle to Salvation, being a Manual of Buddhist Monism" in <u>Acta Orientalia</u>, Vol. IX, 1930-31. 81ff.
24. Ruegg, <u>A History of Indian Literature</u>, 7.
25. Wing-tsit Chan, <u>A Source Book in Chinese Philosophy</u>. (Princeton: Princeton University Press, 1963) 136.

26. Wing-tsit Chan, 136.
27. Loy, Nonduality, 101.
28. Garfield, 181.
29. The term advaita, according to Grimes, can be translated literally from the Sanskrit as "nondualism." (from *a* = "not" + *dvaita* = "dual, two"). John Grimes, A Concise Dictionary of Indian Philosophy. (New York: State University of New York Press, 1996) 15.
30. Hacker, 137.
31. Hacker, 137-38.
32. David Seyfort Ruegg, "The *Jo Nan Pas*: A School of Buddhist Ontologists according to the *grub mtha' šel gyi me lon*" Journal of the American Oriental Society, Vol. 83, 1963: 73.
33. Ruegg, The *Jo Nan Pas*, 74.
34. Ruegg, The *Jo Nan Pas*, 77.
35. Obermiller, 106-107.
36. J.F. Staal, Advaita and Neoplatonism, Edited by T.M.P. Mahadevan. (Madras: University of Madras, 1961) 243.
37. Staal, Advaita, 235.
38. K. Satchidananda Murty, Nagarjuna. (New Delhi: National Book Trust, 1971) 42.
39. Murty, 6.
40. Lindtner, 9.
41. Lindtner provides other names for this work such as: "*Mādhyamikasūtra, Mādhyamikaśāstra*…or, especially among Tibetans, *rtsa ba šes rab, Mūla-prajñā*, or *Mūlaprakarana*" 24f
42. Lindtner, 24.
43. Garfield, 275.
44. Nagao, 178.
45. Conze, 132.
46. Conze, 132.
47. Paul Williams, Mahāyāna Buddhism: The Doctrinal Foundations. (New York: Routledge, 1989) 71-72.
48. Garfield, 276.
49. Garfield, 275-76.
50. Loy, Nonduality, 17.

51. Loy, Nonduality, 4.
52. Loy, Nonduality, 5.
53. Loy, Nonduality, 5.
54. Loy, Nonduality, 5.
55. Lindtner, 269.
56. Lindtner, 269-70.
57. Lindtner, 269.
58. Loy, Nonduality, 17.
59. Loy, Nonduality, 11.
60. In it original context, David Loy describes this aspect of nonduality as "the possibility of a mystical unity between God and man" (Nonduality, 17). In the broader discussion that he embarks upon, this language seems reasonable and, perhaps, even necessary. However, I have experienced difficulties with the use of these terms in the context of this thesis and find it desirable to acquire other terms more suitable for the present context. For the term 'man' I have decided to simply rely upon the more generic and less gendered term 'individual'. The word 'God', however, presents me with a much greater challenge. In its original context, I interpret the word God, as used by Loy, to represent that ultimate creative force from which human beings feel fundamentally separated, divorced, or alienated, and to which all of their religious or mystical efforts, over countless millennia, have been aimed. Whether such efforts have been toward the appeasement or satisfaction of this ultimate creative force, or simply toward establishing a degree of harmony with it, it has most assuredly reflected a need to obtain a closer relationship to it. In Buddhist dictum, I have chosen the term 'Absolute' to reflect this thought.
61. Nagao, 214.
62. Kamaleswar Bhattacharya, The Dialectical Method of Nāgārjuna. (Delhi: Motilal Banarsidass, 1978) 1-2.
63. Bhattacharya, 1.

Nonduality – The Negation of Dualist Thinking

64. Nagao, 214.
65. Loy, Nonduality, 18.
66. David Loy provides an in-depth discussion on *lack* and its effect on Western society in his newest publication, A Buddhist History of the West: Studies in Lack (New York: State University of New York Press, 2002). See also his earlier book Lack and Transcendence: The Problem of Death and Life in Psychotherapy, Existentialism, and Buddhism. (New York: Humanity Books, 1996). Finally, a substantial amount of related material on this topic can be found in two books by Ernest Becker: Escape From Evil (New York: The Free Press, 1975), and the Pulitzer Prize winning The Denial of Death (New York: The Free Press, 1973).
67. Christmas Humphreys, Studies in the Middle Way. (London: Curzon Press, 1976) 123.
68. Garfield, 287.
69. Nagao, 212.
70. Nagao, 213.
71. Garfield, 105.
72. David J. Kalupahana, Mulamadhyamakakārikā of Nāgārjuna: The Philosophy of the Middle Way. (Delhi: Motilal Banarsidass Publishers, 1986) 32. Garfield also agrees with this interpretation, 103-7.
73. Garfield, 105.
74. Garfield, 105.
75. Garfield, 105.
76. Garfield, 105.
77. Garfield, 113.
78. Garfield, 118-19.
79. Garfield, 118.
80. Garfield, 116.
81. Garfield, 121-22.
82. Nagao, 43.
83. Garfield, 281.

Nonduality – The Nonplurality of the World

84. Loy, Nonduality, 21.
85. Loy, Nonduality, 23.
86. See, for instance, Upanisads, translated by Patrick Olivelle (Oxford: Oxford University Press, 1996) 238, 246.
87. Loy, Nonduality, 25.
88. Garfield, 286.
89. Garfield, 286.
90. Garfield, 276.
91. Garfield, 276-77.
92. Garfield, 277.
93. Garfield, 277.
94. Garfield, 277.
95. Garfield, 277.
96. Garfield, 277.
97. Kalupahana, 305.
98. Kalupahana, 305.
99. Garfield, 277.
100. Richard Wolheim, F. H. Bradley (Harmondsworth: Penguin Books Ltd., 1959) 190-1.
101. F.H. Bradley, Appearance and Reality. (Oxford: Oxford University Press, 1978) 26.
102. Wollheim, 193.
103. Wollheim, 105.
104. Fernando Tola and Carmen Dragonetti, On Voidness: A Study on Buddhist Nihilism. Edited by Alex Wayman. (Delhi: Motilal Banarsidass Publishers, 1995) xv.
105. Victor Mansfield, "Relativity in Maadhyamika Buddhism and Modern Physics" Philosophy East and West. Volume 40, no. 1, January 1990. 60-61.

Nonduality – The Nondifference of Subject and Object

106. Susumu Yamaguchi, <u>Mahāyāna Way to Buddhahood</u>. (Los Angeles: Buddhist Books International, 1982) 27.
107. <u>The Dhammapada</u>. Translated by Juan Mascaró. (New York: Penguin Books, 1973) 36.
108. <u>Upanisads</u>, 30.
109. <u>Upanisads</u>. 68.
110. Garfield, 91-92.
111. Garfield, 91-92.
112. Garfield, 93.
113. Garfield, 92.
114. Garfield, 179.
115. Garfield, 179.
116. Garfield, 184-85.
117. Garfield, 185.
118. Garfield, 182.
119. Garfield, 182.
120. Garfield, 92.
121. Garfield, 220.
122. Garfield, 221.
123. Garfield, 221.

Nonduality – The Identity of Phenomenon and the Absolute

124. Garfield, 220.
125. Garfield, 92.
126. Loy, <u>Nonduality</u>, 11.
127. Garfield, 330.
128. Loy, <u>Nonduality</u>, 12.
129. Loy, <u>Nonduality</u>, 249.
130. As we will come to see in the next chapter, this point has a powerful soteriological implication.
131. Loy, <u>Nonduality</u>, 11.
132. Donald S. Lopez, Jr., <u>A Study of Svātantrika</u>. (New York: Snow Lion Publications, 1987) 39.

133. Nagao, 42.
134. Nagao, 15.
135. Loy, Nonduality, 249.
136. Garfield, 249-51.
137. Garfield, 331.
138. Garfield, 331.
139. Ian Charles Harris, The Continuity of Madhyamaka and Yogācāra in Indian Mahāyāna Buddhism. (New York: E. J. Brill, 1991) 2.
140. Garfield, 332.

Nonduality – A Mystical Union Between the Individual and the Absolute

141. Nagao, 160.
142. The word reification is appropriate here and comes from the Latin root *res* meaning 'a thing.' Reification, then, is described as an activity to "convert mentally into a thing" or "to materialize." It is in this activity of interpreting reality in terms of 'things,' particularly when it comes to developing concepts about oneself, that we become conditioned by conventional truth.
143. Garfield, 338.
144. Garfield, 182.
145. G. M. Nagao, *"What Remains" in Śūnyatā*, Mahāyāna Buddhist Meditation: Theory and Practice. Edited by Minoru Kiyota. (Honolulu: University Press of Hawaii, 1978) 77.
146. Nagao, *What Remains*, 69.
147. Nagao, *What Remains*, 78.
148. Nagao, *What Remains*, 77.
149. Nagao, *What Remains*, 77.
150. Loy, Lack, xiv.
151. José Ignacio Cabezón, A Dose of Emptiness: An Annotated Translation of the *sTong thun chen mo* of

mKhas grub dGe legs dpal bzang. (Delhi: Sri Satguru Publications, 1992) 128.
152. Loy, Lack, xv.
153. Garfield, 332.
154. Garfield, 332-33.
155. Garfield, 319.
156. Garfield, 330.
157. Garfield, 334.
158. Garfield, 339-40.

Parallels between the Mūlamadhyamakakārikā and Quantum Physics

159. The Book of Kindred Saying (Sanyutta-nikāya). Translated by Mrs. Rhys Davids and F.H. Woodward. (Oxford: The Pali Text Society, 1997) 25.
160. Fritjof Capra, The Tao of Physics. (London: Flamingo, 1975) 337-38.
161. Shimon Malin, Nature Loves to Hide. (Oxford, Oxford University Press, 2001) xiv.
162. David Z. Albert, Quantum Mechanics and Experience. (Cambridge: Harvard University Press, 1992) 59-60.
163. David Bohm, Wholeness and the Implicate Order. (New York: Routledge, 1980) 199.
164. Bohm, 149.
165. Bohm, 134.
166. Werner Heisenberg, Physics and Philosophy: The Revolution in Modern Science. (New York: Prometheus Books, 1958) 160.
167. Henry Stapp, Mind, Matter, and Quantum Mechanics. (New York: Springer-Verlag, 1993) 83.
168. Stapp, p. 136.
169. Stapp, p. 136.
170. Euan Squires, Conscious Mind in the Physical World. (Philadelphia: Institute of Physics Publishing, 1990) 205.

171. Amit Goswami, The Self-Aware Universe. (New York: Penguin Putnam Inc., 1993) 11.
172. Steven Kaufman, Unified Reality Theory: The Evolution of Existence Into Experience. (Milwaukee: Destiny Toad Press, 2002) 166.
173. Garfield, 184-85.
174. Kaufman, 166,
175. Paul Davies, God and the New Physics. (New York: Simon & Schuster, 1983) 102.
176. Garfield, 133.
177. Davies, 103.
178. Menas Kafatos and Robert Nadeau, The Conscious Universe. (New York: Springer, 1990) 10.
179. Many interesting parallels will be found between the ideas of a universal matrix and the Buddhist story of Indra's jeweled net. David Loy's provides an interesting discussion on this in "Indra's Postmodern Net", Philosophy East and West, Volume 43, no. 3, 1983: 481-510.
180. Kaufman, 166.
181. Arnold Mindell, Quantum Mind: The Edge Between Physics and Psychology. (Portland: Lao Tse Press, 2000) 247.
182. This concept, discussed by one of psychology's most prominent historical figures, still remains virtually untested and unexamined throughout the whole of the orthodox scientific community.
183. Mindell, 240.
184. Kaufman, p. 167.
185. Kaufman, p. 166.
186. Kaufman, 169.
187. Kaufman, 169.
188. Kaufman, 169.
189. Kaufman, 169.
190. Kaufman, 169.
191. See Florin Giripescu Sutton's interesting discussion of the development of logical methods, East and West, in

Existence and Enlightenment in the Laṅkāvatāra-sūtra. (New York: State University of New York Press, 1991) 135-67.
192. Alfred North Whitehead, Process and Reality. Corrected Edition. (New York: The Free Press, 1978) 4.
193. John D. Barrow, Impossibility: The Limits of Science and the Science of Limits. (Oxford: Oxford University Press, 1998) ix.
194. Sutton, 140.
195. It should be noted that some early Buddhist philosophers even employed a sixfold combination of 'is/is not' called the septalemma. While this formula does make subtler arguments regarding existence, it makes no new propositions. That is, it merely extends the use of the previous four propositions of the tetralemma in unique and interesting combinations.
196. Nagao, 179.
197. Sutton, 140.
198. Albert, 11.
199. The 'material' self, apart from the physical body of the individual, includes emotions, feelings, sensations, and thoughts. This is in line with the Buddhist view of the *skandhas*.

Bibliography

Abram, David. The Spell of the Sensuous. New York: Vintage Books, 1996.

Albert, David Z. Quantum Mechanics and Experience. Cambridge: Harvard University Press, 1992.

Barrow, John D. Impossibility: The Limits of Science and the Science of Limits. Oxford: Oxford University Press, 1998.

Becker, Ernest. The Denial of Death. New York: The Free Press, 1973.

---- Escape From Evil. New York: The Free Press, 1975.

Bhattacharya, Kamaleswar. The Dialectical Method of Nāgārjuna. Delhi: Motilal Banarsidass, 1978.

Bohm, David. Wholeness and the Implicate Order. New York: Routledge, 1980.

Bradley, F. H. Appearance and Reality. Oxford: Oxford University Press, 1978.

Cabezón, José Ignacio. A Dose of Emptiness: An Annotated Translation of the sTong thun chen mo of mKhas grub dGe legs dpal bzang. Delhi: Sri Satguru Publications, 1992.

Capra, Fritjof. The Tao of Physics. London: Flamingo, 1975.

Conze, Edward. Buddhism: Its Essence and Development. New York: Harper & Row Publishers, 1959.

Davies, Paul. God and the New Physics. New York: Simon & Schuster, 1983.

Dhammapada, The. Translated by Juan Mascaró. New York: Penguin Books, 1973.

Dossey, Larry. Recovering the Soul: A Scientific and Spiritual Search. New York: Bantam, 1989

---- Reinventing Medicine: Beyond Mind-Body to a New Era of Healing. San Francisco:Harper, 2000.

Frauwallner, Erich. History of Indian Philosophy. Delhi: Motilal Banarsidass, 1973.

Friedman, Norman. Bridging Science and Spirit. St. Louis: Living Lake Books, 1990.

Garfield, Jay. The Fundamental Wisdom of the Middle Way: Nāgārjuna's *Mūlamadhyamakakārikā*. New York: Oxford University Press, 1995.

Grimes, John. A Concise Dictionary of Indian Philosophy. New York: State of New York Press, 1996.

Goswami, Amit. The Self-Aware Universe. New York: Penguin Putnam Inc., 1993.

Hacker, Paul. Philology and Confrontation. Edited by Wilhelm Halbfass. New York: State University of New York Press, 1995.

Harris, Ian Charles. The Continuity of Madhyamaka and Yogācāra in Indian Mahāyāna Buddhism. New York: E. J. Brill, 1991.

Heisenberg, Werner. Physics and Philosophy: The Revolution in Modern Science. New York: Prometheus Books, 1958.

Bibliography

Herbert, Nick. Quantum Reality. New York: Doubleday, 1987.

---- Elemental Mind. New York: Dutton, 1993.

Humphreys, Christmas. Studies in the Middle Way. London: Curzon Press, 1976.

Kafatos, Menas and Nadeau, Robert. The Conscious Universe. New York: Springer, 1990.

Kalupahana, David J. Mulamadhyamakakārikā of Nāgārjuna: The Philosophy of the Middle Way. Delhi: Motilal Banarsidass Publishers, 1986.

Kaufman, Steven. Unified Reality Theory: The Evolution of Existence Into Experience. Milwaukee: Destiny Toad Press, 2002.

Lawlis, G. Frank. Transpersonal Medicine. Boston: Shambhala, 1996.

Lindtner, Christian. Nagarjuniana: Studies in the Writings and Philosophy of Nāgārjuna. Delhi: Motilal Banarsidass, 1982.

---- Journal of the American Oriental Society, vol. 108, 1988: 178.

Lopez, Donald S., Jr. A Study of Svātantrika. New York: Snow Lion Publications, 1987.

Loy, David. "Indra's Postmodern Net", Philosophy East and West, Volume 43, no. 3, 1983: 481-510.

---- Nonduality: A Study in Comparative Philosophy. New York: Humanity Books, 1988.

---- Lack and Transcendence: The Problem of Death and Life in Psychotherapy, Existentialism, and Buddhism. New York: Humanity Books, 1996.

---- A Buddhist History of the West: Studies in Lack Albany: State University of New York Press, 2002.

Malin, Shimon. Nature Loves to Hide. Oxford, Oxford University Press, 2001.

Mansfield, Victor. "Relativity in Maadhyamika Buddhism and Modern Physics" Philosophy East and West. Volume 40, no. 1, January 1990. p. 59-72.

---- Synchronicity, Science, and Soul-Making: Understanding Jungian Synchronicity through Physics, Buddhism, and Philosophy. La Salle, Illinois: Open Court Publishing, 1995.

Mindell, Arnold. Quantum Mind: The Edge Between Physics and Psychology. Portland: Lao Tse Press, 2000.

Murty, K. Satchidananda. Nagarjuna. New Delhi: National Book Trust, 1971.

Nagao, G. M. *"What Remains"* in Śūnyatā, Mahāyāna Buddhist Meditation: Theory and Practice. Edited by Minoru Kiyota. Honolulu: University Press of Hawaii, 1978.

---- Mādhyamika and Yogācāra: A Study of Mahāyāna Philosophies. Delhi: Sri Satguru Publications, 1991.

Obermiller, E. "The Sublime Science of the Great Vehicle to Salvation, being a Manual of Buddhist Monism" in Acta Orientalia, Vol. IX, 1930-31. 81-306.

Ruegg, David Seyfort. "The *Jo Nan Pas*: A School of Buddhist Ontologists according to the *grub mtha' šel gyi me lon*" Journal of the American Oriental Society, Vol. 83, 1963: 73-91.

Bibliography

---- A History of Indian Literature: The Literature of the Madhyamaka School of Philosophy in India. Wiesbaden: Harrasowitz, 1981.

Samuel, Geoffrey. Civilized Shamans: Buddhism in Tibetan Societies. Washington: Smithsonian Institution Press, 1993.

Singh, Jaidev. An Introduction to Madhyamaka Philosophy. Delhi: Motilal Banarsidass, 1968.

Squires, Euan. Conscious Mind in the Physical World. Philadelphia: Institute of Physics Publishing, 1990.

Staal, J.F. Advaita and Neoplatonism. Edited by T.M.P. Mahadevan. Madras: University of Madras, 1961.

Stapp, Henry. Mind, Matter, and Quantum Mechanics. New York: Springer-Verlag, 1993.

Sutton, Florin Giripescu. Existence and Enlightenment in the Laṅkāvatāra-sūtra. New York: State University of New York Press, 1991.

The Book of Kindred Saying (Sanyutta-nikāya). Translated by Mrs. Rhys Davids and F.H. Woodward. Oxford: The Pali Text Society, 1997.

Tola, Fernando and Carmen Dragonetti, On Voidness: A Study on Buddhist Nihilism. Edited by Alex Wayman. Delhi: Motilal Banarsidass Publishers, 1995.

Upanisads, The. Translated by Patrick Olivelle. Oxford: Oxford University Press, 1996.

Whitehead, Alfred North. Process and Reality. Corrected Edition. New York: The Free Press, 1978.

Wilbur, Ken. Sex, Ecology, Spirituality. Boston: Shambhala, 1995.

Williams, Paul. Mahāyāna Buddhism: The Doctrinal Foundations. New York: Routledge, 1989.

Wing-tsit Chan, A Source Book in Chinese Philosophy. Princeton: Princeton University Press, 1963.

Wisdom of the Buddha: The Unabridged Dhammapada. Edited and translated by F. Max Müller. New York: Dover Publications, Inc., 2000.

Wolf, Fred Alan. Taking the Quantum Leap. New York: Harper & Row, 1981.

Wollheim, Richard. F. H. Bradley. Harmondsworth: Penguin Books Ltd., 1959.

Yamaguchi, Susumu. Mahāyāna Way to Buddhahood. Los Angeles: Buddhist Books International, 1982.

www.ingramcontent.com/pod-product-compliance
Lightning Source LLC
Chambersburg PA
CBHW020804160426
43192CB00006B/437